Wendy Susan Deaton, MA, MFT
Michael Hertica, MS, MFT

Manual para Sobrevivientes de la Violencia Doméstica

Pre-publication
REVIEWS,
COMMENTARIES,
EVALUATIONS . . .

"**A**s a nurse educator, I will make *Growing Free* required reading for nursing students at all levels of education. Nurses are in a unique position to intervene in domestic violence. Simply giving this manual to a client who seems to be suffering in a relationship would be a powerful thing to do. Reading this text may also give some students insight into their own experiences and encourage them to apply the authors' suggestions to circumstances in which they can identify coercion, verbal abuse, or humiliation—whether at work, in training, or in their family."

Beatrice Crofts Yorker, RN, JD
Professor of Nursing,
Georgia State University,
Decatur

"**I**n *Growing Free,* the authors have captured the essence of what survivors really need—recognition of their struggle, information on the big picture, and clear options about what they can do now. The simple outline of safety plans under a variety of conditions makes a complex subject manageable. Most important, the authors address the 'how to' of rebuilding one's life.

This is a necessary book for anyone who is scared and starting to think about what it would take to 'grow free.' Friends and relatives of a person in a domestic violence situation can use this very helpful book as a guide. I recommend it highly."

Colleen Friend, LCSW
Field Work Consultant,
UCLA Department
of Social Welfare,
School of Public Policy
& Social Research

Creciendo Libre
Manual para Sobrevivientes de la Violencia Doméstica

THE HAWORTH MALTREATMENT AND TRAUMA PRESS®
Robert A. Geffner, PhD
Senior Editor

Creciendo Libre
Manual para Sobrevivientes de la Violencia Doméstica

Wendy Susan Deaton, MA, MFT
Michael Hertica, MS, MFT

Traducido por
Christell J. Quinche, MA

The Haworth Maltreatment and Trauma Press®
An Imprint of The Haworth Press, Inc.
New York • London • Oxford

Published by

The Haworth Maltreatment and Trauma Press®, an imprint of The Haworth press, Inc., 10 Alice
Street, Binghamton, NY 13904-1580.

Cover design by Jennifer M. Gaska.

Library of Congress Cataloging-in-Publication Data

Deaton, Wendy.
  [Growing free. Spanish]
  Creciendo libre : manual para sobrevivientes de la violencia doméstica / Wendy Susan Deaton,
Michael Hertica ; traducido por Christell J. Quinche.
    p. cm.
  ˙Translation of: Growing free.
  Includes index.
  ISBN 0-7890-1899-3 (soft : alk. paper)
  1. Family violence—Psychological aspects. 2. Victims of family violence—Psychology.
I. Hertica, Michael. II. Title.
HV6626.D4318 2003
362.82'924—dc22
                                                                                            2003017539

Para Summer y Heather
Que sus futuros sean libres de violencia
y llena de serenidad.
Quien las quiere, Nana

Para 1736,
Nicole y Curtis,
Gracias, Mike

CONTENIDO

SOBRE LOS AUTORES

Wendy Susan Deaton, MA, MFT, ha tenido su licenciatura en terapia matrimonial y familiar y a brindado estos servicios en su consultorio privado desde 1982. Ella ha trabajado extensamente en el área de victimizacion y abuso, incluyendo tratamiento individual y entrenamientos a la policía, abogados, trabajadores sociales, personal de alberges, proveedores de servicio medico y psicológico. Publicaciones profesionales escritos por Wendy incluye dos ediciones de *Child Sexual Abuse Dispute Annotated Bibliography* y los *Manuales de Crecimiento y Recuperación (Growth and Recovery Workbooks),* una serie de artículos terapéuticos para niños. *Crecimiento y Recuperación* incluye una serie de manuales dedicados a como vivir bajo la violencia doméstica, abuso sexual, y otros tipos de traumas presenciados y vividos por los niños. Sus artículos profesionales han aparecido en al *CAPSAC Consultant,* el *ASPAC Advisor,* y en el *Nurse Practioner Forum.* Ella ha sido parte de la Junta de Directores de la Sociedad Profesional de California en el Abuso de Niños (CAPSAC) desde 1993.

Teniente Michael Hertica, MS, MFT, se retiro del Departamento de Policia donde trabajo desde 1969-1999. Teniente Hertica es un instructor en la investigación de abuso de nios y casos de violencia doméstica. El ha entrenado en conferencias y para agencias por todo el mundo. Sus temas de instrucción incluyen como el Entrevistar Niños y Adolescentes; Entrevistar y Tomar el Perfil de Ofensores; Investigación de Abuso de Niños; y Violencia Doméstica y los Efectos en los Niños. El teniente Hertica ha publicado artículos de abuso de niños en la revista *The Police Chief,* el *FBI Law Enforcement Bulletin,* y el *APSAC Advisor.* El es el antiguo presidente de la Junta de Directores de la Sociedad Profesional de California en el Abuso de Niños. El tiene su licenciatura en conserjería matrimonial y familiar. El actualmente trabaja para El Centro de Crisis Familiar 1736, un refugio de violencia doméstica y un programa para los adolescentes en Redondo Beach, California.

Traductor

Christell J. Quinche, MA, es una estudiante de psicologia clinica de la universidad Alliant International University en San Diego, California. En el transcurso de su preparación, ella se a especializado como facilitadora de grupos para hombres y mujeres ofensores y victimas de violencia doméstica. Ella ha adquirido diversos entrenamientos y se destaca en poder ofrecer un servicio a la comunidad Hispana en el condado de San Diego.

Prólogo

Este programa refleja una combinación de nuestras experiencias en los papeles que desenvolvemos como consejero y oficial de policía. Por lo tanto, ni el manual ni la guía del terapeuta contiene notas en el pie de páen gina o referencias de otros trabajos. Un capítulo de introducción acompaña la guía del terapeuta, citados en algunas investigaciones y estudios que han surgido durante los últimos 25 años que valida y apoya nuestra propia perspectiva sobre la Violencia Familiar.

El manual provee un esquema para el sobreviviente, para ayudarle en la evaluación de sus relaciones presentes, pasadas, o futuras con el fin de que pueda sanar y luego evitar los efectos destructivos de la violencia doméstica.

El manual no fue elaborado para completar el proceso de sanidad, fue hecho para ser utilizado durante un proceso de crecimiento y cambio por lo cual usted podrá buscar otras vías de información, guía y apoyo. Nosotros animamos a localizar un terapeuta que sea entrenado específicamente en la violencia doméstica, y que demuestre una actitud de paciencia, compasión y ante todo "respeto." El terapeuta podrá tener sus propios deseos para su futuro, pero el o ella deberá poner esos deseos a un lado, y por el contrario, asistirle en el desarrollo de sus propias metas. No es responsabilidad del terapeuta tomar decisiones por el mismo o tomar alguna acción por usted; es responsabilidad del terapeuta apoyarle en su crecimiento para que pueda tomar sus propias decisiones y elegir las acciones que sean correctas. El terapeuta debera proveer información y recursos que incluyan el acudir a otros sistemas de apoyo tales como los grupos de auto-ayuda y terapia en grupo, asistencia policial y servicios legales. El papel de un terapeuta es servir como guía en su jornada, ayudándole en los obstáculos del camino, y aplaudiendo cuando exitosamente logra negociar las dificultades y las vueltas de la vida.

Sea cual sea el resultado de su trabajo, es nuestra esperanza y deseo que este manual le sirva de compañia y que le anime a permanecer siempre segura y valorandose a si misma.

Wendy Susan Deaton
Michael Hertica

Capítulo 1

¿Soy Yo?

- ¿Está usted en una relación y aún se siente aislada y sola?
- ¿Cree qué es culpa suya si su pareja no es feliz?
- ¿Cree qué su pareja solo se enoja porque la quiere?
- ¿Cree qué las críticas de su pareja son solo para ayudarle?
- ¿Su pareja abusó de usted física o emocionalmente?
- ¿Siente que usted o sus hijos corren algun peligro si usted decide salirse de la relación?
- ¿Está en un rehén emocional?
- ¿Teme que no pueda sobrevivir sola?
- ¿Cree que si solo usted cambiará, su pareja cambiará?

Si has respondido si a cualquiera de estas preguntas,
¡Este libro es para ti!

De vez en cuando, todos hemos tenido uno o dos de estos pensamientos, pero si los ha tenido frecuentemente, usted puede ser una víctima de violencia doméstica. Al ser una víctima, usted puede creer ser responsable por causar o por controlar todo lo que pasa en su relación. Puede creer que los problemas en la relación son su culpa. Usted podrá racionalizar, minimizar o justificar el comportamiento de su pareja, y tomar toda la responsabilidad por la violencia. Tomar responsabilidad ofrece un sentimiento de poder y control sobre situaciones que son atemorizantes y abrumadoras. Sin embargo, hay maneras saludables para sentir control sin tratar de manejar o cambiar sentimientos, creencias, y los comportamientos de su pareja.

¿QUE ES LA VIOLENCIA DOMÉSTICA?

La violencia doméstica incluye violencia física, abuso emocional, económico, sexual, intimidación y el uso de los niños para adquirir poder y control. Toda relación es única y es compuesta de diferentes tipos de comportamientos. Una relación puede ser abusiva sin violencia física. Algunas relaciones puede incluir solo amenazas, culpabilidad, e intimidación. Algunos incluyen solo un tipo de comportamiento abusivo. La mayoría de las relaciones abusivas de cualquier manera, incluyen varios tipos de consecuencias perjudiciales.

La violencia doméstica puede sucederle a cualquiera. Puede occurir en familias de diversas razas, colores, religiones y niveles socioeconómicos. Ocurre en todas las edades, en todos los niveles educativos y en diferentes relaciones sexuales. Aunque algunos estudios sugieren que el abuso y los comportamientos violentos ocurren muy frecuentemente en bajo niveles socioeconómicos, teniendo establidad economica o riquezas no lo hace exempto el abuso. La violencia doméstica también puede ocurrir en su propia familia. Para facilitar la lectura, hemos usado el pronombre femenino para hablar sobre las victimas, pero por favor: recuerde que el hombre también puede ser victima de la violencia doméstica.

DEFINICIONES DE LA VIOLENCIA EN LA RELACIONES

1. La violencia física incluye: tirar objetos, empujar, pegar, patear o cualquier otra actividad física que pueda causar algún daño físico.
2. Abuso verbal y abuso emocional incluye: el hacer que se sienta mal de si misma, el decirle nombres ofensivos, hacerla pensar que ha enloquecido, aislándola de sus amistades y seres queridos, culpándola y utilizando otro tipos de "juegos mentales."
3. Abuso económico incluye: se genera con la dependencia económica, sin posibilidades de conseguir trabajo y quitándole acceso al dinero y a sus pertenecías.
4. Abuso sexual incluye: ataques físicos que involucre partes intimas de su cuerpo o forzándole a tener relaciones sexuales contra su voluntad.
5. Intimidación incluye amenazas, gritos, ignorándole, o actuando en maneras violentas enfrente de usted como perforar la pared, romper sus cosas personales, o lastimando a su mascota.
6. Usando a los niños para adquirir poder y control incluye amenazas para quitar la custodia de los niños, privar a sus niños de apoyo económico, o registrando reportes negativos o falsos hacia la policía, servicios sociales, o a la corte.

Estas no son las únicas maneras que se pueda expresar la violencia doméstica, pero son las que occure con más frecuencia. *Si ha tenido alguna de estas experiencias, usted necesita continuar leyendo este libro.* No existe una solución fácil en las relaciones, y es particularmente cierto en las relaciones donde existe violencia y abuso. Si estás en una relación violenta, este libro no será la respuesta a todos sus problemas. Al contrario, este libro puede servir como un amigo o una guía. Ofrece información de como llego a la relación, como le ha afectado a usted y a sus hijos, y como podrá empezar a tomar, decisiones benéficas en su vida. Le ayudará a ver patrones en su pensar, sentir y actuar que le han conducido a elegir la relación, a la vez le demostrará los patrones que son perjudiciales para usted y sus seres queridos. También le ayudará a encontrar diferentes maneras de ver la vida, y otras opciones y decisiones que puede tomar.

Este libro es para cualquiera que ha estado en una relación que lo ha hecho sentir mal de si mismo, en una relación en la cual no recibió el amor o el respeto que merecía, o en el que fue abusada. Es también un libro para profesionales que trabajan con personas que han estado o están en relaciones de esta indole.

ACEPTANDO DONDE ESTAS

Al leer este libro, usted ya esta tomando el primer pasó hacia el cambio en su vida. Leer este libro significa que usted esta confrontando las preguntas y las preocupaciones que con lleva reconocer que su relacion no es saludable.

El próximo paso en como cambiar su vida incluye el hacerse algunas preguntas importantes.

- ¿Está lista a renunciar su auto-negación y confrontar el problema de violencia en su relación?
- ¿Está lista para admitir que está pasando por una relación dolorosa aunque no quiera salir de ella?
- ¿Está lista para aceptar que su relación ha tenido un impacto negativo en usted y en sus niños?
- ¿Está lista para aceptar que aunque no haya recibido abuso físico en su relación esto no le garantiza que las amenazas vayan a terminar?

Su antepasado pudo haberla preparado a estar en una relación enfermiza o peligrosa. Muchos adultos que viven en una relación abusiva o violenta han anteriormente experimentado algún tipo de abuso o negligencia en su niñez. Si usted fue abusada cuando niña, probablemente aprendió a creer que el abuso fue por su culpa.

El padre de Raelyn era físicamente y sexualmente abusivo. Cuando le pegaba o abusaba sexualmente de ella, el le decía que ella estaba siendo castigada por ser una "niña mala." Que el abuso pararía siempre en cuando ella llegara aprender a "como comportarse." Raelyn le creyó a su padre. Ella creyó que era responsable por su comportamiento. Cuando adulta, sin entender porque, ella siempre buscaba relaciones en la cual ella recibiría aprobación por ser una "niña buena." Raelyn buscó parejas que le acordaran a su padre-parejas abusivas -y después ella trataba de utilizar diferentes tipos de comportamientos para lograr detener la situación. Por causa de las creencias de su infancia, Raelyn no pudo entender que el abuso en la relación no era resultado de su comportamiento sino al contrario, que era el resultado de haber elegido una pareja abusiva.

Cuando niña le pudieron haber enseñado que el abuso formaba parte de una relación normal.

Sherri se crió en una familia extensa, con muchos tíos, primos, y hermanos. En la familia de Sherri, las mujeres eran ciudadanas de segunda clase; ellas existían para servir al hombre. El padre y los tíos de Sherri establecían todas las reglas. Sherri no podía tener amistades fuera de la escuela o visitar a sus compañeras. Ella no tenia oportunidad de ver familias donde no había abuso. Las mujeres en la familia de Sherri eran menospreciadas, maltratadas, golpeadas y culpadas por todo lo malo que ocurría. Sherri pensó que así operaban todas las familias—que ser una víctima era el papel que la mujer comunmente desenvolvia.

El cerebro de un niño no esta completamente desarrollado. El desarrollo del cerebro en un niño causa que vea el mundo diferente. No como un adulto suele ver al mundo. Los niños creen que son el centro del mundo, en vez de entender que el mundo existe inde-pendientemente de ellos. Ellos no entienden que otras personas y otras circunstancias tienen influencia sobre las situaciones que ellos experimentan. Experiencias que apoyan las creencias de un niño causan que todo sea fácilmente aceptado, mientras que otras experiencias demuestran que su poder e influencia en el mundo es en verdad limitado. Esto no tiene mucho sentido para una pequeña criatura. Las creencias de un niño las cuales, son muy fuertes en ciertas situaciones de la vida, llegan a convencerlos facilmente que ellos tienen la culpa de todo lo que pasa.

Si usted crece creyendo que es culpable del abuso que sufrio cuando niña, o que el abuso es normal, cargara estas creencias hasta que sea adulta. Las experiencias de la niñez son las más poderosas de todas a medida que vas creciendo. Lo que aprendes en la vida después de la niñez puede que no sea tan real o tan verdadero como han sido sus primeras experiencias.

Por ejemplo, imagine un círculo. Dentro del círculo esta todas sus experiencias de la infancia—todas sus memorias, pensamientos, y sentimientos. De estas experiencias, construye el punto de vista del mundo y lo que le rodea. Experiencias que vienen después aparecen como anillos alrededor del círculo original de sus creencias, y todo lo que ocurre después es influenciado por el punto de vista que usted trazo anteriormente.

Si en su infancia usted fue una niña protegida y querida, usted ingresa ra a la escuela y al mundo social, esperando ser tratada de la misma manera. A usted le atrae ra personas que son nobles, cariñosos, y que les de aprobación. Si la mayoría de sus experiencias son de dolor, negligencia y rechazo, por más que no le guste ser herida usted aprendera a esperar lo mismo de los otros y se encontrara atraída hacia personas negligentes y abusivas. Aunque después pueda tener otras experiencias positivas en su vida, estas experiencias no son parte de sus creencias y puede que ellos nunca sean lo suficientemente poderosas en influenciar sus decisiones. Entre mas temprano llegues a la conclusión de quien eres y como es el mundo, mas fuerte va ser el que esas creencias moldean sus futuras decisiones, especialmente cuando se trata de escoger una pareja.

Aunque en su niñez no haya podido entender que usted no era la culpable del abuso, como adulta, usted podra aprender que no es responsable por los sentimientos, actitudes, comportamientos, o las acciones cometidas por los demás.

Cuando uno es victima del abuso, siendo niño o adulto, es natural generar excusas por los comportamientos de esas personas. Es difícil aceptar que la persona que uno ama, y quien dice amarla, le pueda herir. Es más fácil racionalizar y tratar de encontrar razones que justifiquen porque la otra persona se comporto de una manera irrazonable o heriente. Es mas fácil creer que el problema, error, y la culpa es suya; piensas que debes de ser ignorante, estupida o torpe, tal como suele decir su pareja. Cuando racionalizas o justificas a la otra persona y sientes culpabilidad, es mas fácil seguir queriendo y creyendo que eres amada.

El presentar excusas por la otra persona y tomar responsabilidad por la violencia o el abuso puede llegar a ser algo muy peligroso. Este tipo de pensamiento puede carcomer su autoestima y auto valor, causando que pierda respeto a si misma. Al pensar que eres la culpable puedas que no estes protegida ante un comportamiento peligroso y que resulte en una relación que no sea saludable y aun muy peligrosa.

Usted no es responsable por el comportamiento de los demás. El comportamiento es una elección individual, una decisión consciente y nunca debe de hacer excusas para que alguien la lastime, emocionalmente o físicamente—"no existe razon alguna" y ninguna explicación seria razonable. Usted crea excusas por el comportamiento de su pareja porque eso es lo que ha aprendido hacer. Cuando inventa excusas, usted evade el confrontar sus propios temores de huir y la confusión de como va a manejar la situación sola. Usted huye aceptando que su relación no va funcionar. Si usted cree que el comportamiento violento resulta de algo que está haciendo, podrá continuar creyendo que cambiando su propio comportamiento cambiará el comportamiento de su pareja. Creando excusas y tomando culpa le hace creer que tiene el control. Que usted puede cambiar lo que está pasando al solo cambiar su propio comportamiento.

Usted puede intentar otras maneras de evadir el confrontar su dolor de admitir que esta en una relación peligrosa. A veces podrá olvidar, pretendiendo que la violencia nunca pasó. Alomejor olvidando lo que actualmente se dijo, sucedió, y cuan serio fue el peligro. Si puede olvidar, seguirá pretendiendo, imaginando, deseando, y esperando que todo siga bien. Este tipo de evasión se llama negación. Evadiendo la realidad por medio de la negación es vivir en un mundo de fantasía. Cuando se queda en la negación, usted falla en tomar los pasos necesarios para permanecer segura.

Usted podrá minimizar el comportamiento, decidiendo que no es tan serio como parece. Pensará, "Lo que el dijo en verdad no fue tan doloroso. Yo solo soy muy sensible" o "El en verdad no quiso pegarme; el solo estuvo disgustado. Tan solo fue un accidente." Usted no puede tomar el riesgo de minimizar, racionalizar, o negar. Especialmente no puede arriesgar el olvidar, o es mas seguro para usted, el no olvidar. Debe recordar lo que sucedió. En el fondo, tendrá que dejar que sus recuerdos regresen, no para lastimarla o castigarla, sino como una manera de confrontar la realidad y como medida a mantenerse motivada a crecer y cambiar. Acepte que la violencia es real, que pasó y que tiene que parar.

A medida que empieza a confrontar lo que le está pasando, podrá experimentar muchos sentimientos. Es natural que sienta miedo, pero también comenzarás a sentir la necesidad de tomar una acción, para cambiar la situación. Esto puede hacer que termine la relación, lo cual probablemente tendrá algunas consecuencias importantes. Podrás perder la casa, el apoyo económico provisto por su pareja, y la comodidad de ser casada. Podrá pensar que no remplazará estas cosas o que no podrá sostenerse a si misma o a los niños. Tendras la preocupación de no tener suficiente dinero o un lugar decente para vivir. Puedes pensar que nunca tendrás otra relación, que nunca serias amada, o que siempre estarás sola. Sus temores son normales y naturales, pero usualmente ellos no se hacen una realidad. La mayoría de veces, cuando una persona deja un relación abusiva, encuentra maneras de apoyarse por medio de amistades y profesionales que la pueden ayudar, y—si continúa creciendo y amándose a si misma, encontrara una relación mas saludable. El temor no es una razón para quedarse en una relación infeliz, enfermiza, ni peligrosa.

Otro sentimiento que puedas presenciar es el enojo. Puedes estar enojada consigo misma, con su pareja, con la gente de su pasado, con sus amigos y familiares, o con sus compañeros del trabajo. Usted podrá sentir temor hacia su propio enojo porque le recordara de la violencia, pero si usted no se permite sentirlo, llegará a sentirse impotente y destrozada. Puede que necesite ayuda con su enojo. Un grupo de apoyo o un consejero profesional le podrá ayudar a elegir maneras saludables de reconocer y expresar sus sentimiento sin tener que lastimarse a si misma ni a los demás. Cuando esta trabajando en su enojo, recuerde que no son sus sentimientos de enojo que causan daño o sean peligrosos, sino la manera en que los expresas. El enojo no es un espiral que sale fuera de control; no tiene que hacerle daño a uno mismo ni a los demás. El enojo es un sentimiento natural que experimenta todo ser humano o cuando se enfrenta ante el peligro. En este libro ofrecemos algunas sugerencias constructivas para saber manejar ese enojo.

Si, usted al confrontar lo que está sucediendo decide terminar la relación, ciertamente se sentirá triste y solo. Si eres honesta consigo misma, podrás reconocer que ese sentimiento lo haz llevado por mucho tiempo. No existe situación tan triste o tan sola como es el estar con alguien quien uno ama y no le corresponde. No permitas que la tristeza y sentimientos de soledad sean razón para quedarte en una relación peligrosa. Reconoze que esa tristeza y soledad son reacciones normales hacia la perdida de cualquier relación.

Es possible que desees que esa tristeza o soledad se desvanezca, pero tambien puedes expresar esos sentimientos y tratar de sobrepasarlos. Trata de tomar un tiempo aparte para enfrentar esos sentimientos. Si sientes ganas de llorar, adelante llora. Si la relación no funciono, tienes derecho aun de tener sentimientos al respecto. Estando triste no significa que debes permanecer en esa relación; el hecho que estés sola ahora no significa que siempre estarás sola. Trata esos sentimientos por un tiempo, después podrás ponerlos a un lado y seguir adelante. Si los sentimientos regresan, vuelve a empezar el proceso una vez y otra vez hasta que ya no sientas el dolor.

Finalmente, cuando ya hayas confrontado la decision de tomar los pasos para detener la violencia, podrás sentir un alivio y emoción. Estos sentimientos puede que den vergüenza o incomodidad. Puedes que sientas cierta culpabilidad porque estas feliz que la relación haya terminado. Estos sentimientos también son muy normales y naturales. Puedes que sientas alivio y emoción porque estas haciendo cambios saludables en la vida que traeran mejores tiempos para usted y para sus hijos. Si no sientes alivio y emoción al principio, no es motivo de preocupación. Estos sentimientos vendrán cuando estés preparada a permitir que seas feliz y libre.

Capítulo 2

Los Efectos de la Violencia Doméstica en la Victima

Ciertamente no todas las victimas de violencia doméstica son mujeres, pero si son el porcentaje mas alto. Este capítulo está enfocado en los efectos de la victima, la cual frecuentemente caracteriza a la mujer. Reconocemos, de cualquier manera, que los hombres pueden también ser victimas de la violencia doméstica.

Muchas, si no todas, las víctimas de la violencia doméstica usan la minimización, racionalización, negación o el olvidar para no enfrentar la realidad de su situación.

Billie le dijo a su terapista: "Marco solo me ha pegado una vez en tres años de casados." Después, sin embargo, ella reveló que el mantenía sus finanzas en secreto y hacia que los ingresos de Billie cubrieran los gastos del hogar. Aparte ellos solo tenían relaciones íntimas cuando el quería y aun mas cuando el venía a la casa después de haber salido a tomar "con los amigos." Le gritaba frecuentemente, y ella se propuso a contarle a su terapista, que Marco nunca le pegaba o le gritaba en frente de su hijo Felipe. "Yo lo dejaría si el lo llegara hacer," Billie declaro muy fuertemente. "Mi mamá y papá pasaron por peores ratos que estos y ellos aun siguen juntos después de treinta y cinco años." Billie no pudo ver que ella estaba en una relación donde había violencia doméstica. Al contrario, ella creía, "Marco es el único hombre que en verdad me ha amado."

Billie es un buen ejemplo de como la víctima de violencia puede llegar a minimizar y racionalizar su situación. Billie tenía motivos para querer negar su realidad. Ella creció en una familia donde la violencia fue algo aceptable. Para sentirse cómoda con su pareja ella eligió creer que la violencia era una parte normal de la relación. Ya que no supo quererse de una manera saludable, ella no pudo imaginar que alguien excepto Marco pudiera encontrarla adorable y deseable. El pensar que Marco la queria y la minimización y racionalización constante de su comportamiento violento, Billie llego a creer que estaba "segura" en su matrimonio.

La mayoría de las víctimas de la violencia doméstica se sienten atrapadas y sin esperanza. Aunque ellas pudieron haber vivido esta situación desde antes del matrimonio o de vivir con su pareja, no saben como cambiarla o detenerla. Ellas tienen miedo de dejar la relación porque no saben como podran asegurar a sus hijos, su estabilidad económica y su seguridad física. Se preocupan por lo que otros pensaran (especialmente si se separan) lo que pensará su familia. No se sienten con la confianza de poder cubrir sus necesidades diarias. Estos temores y preocupaciones conducen a que ellos se queden en una situación violenta por más que sus vidas estén corriendo peligro. Muchas veces se quedan en la relación aunque finalmente hayan reconocido que son infelices y están en peligro.

Las relaciones que contienen violencia doméstica se tornan de muchas maneras. La relación puede contener todo o solo parte de los siguientes elementos: celos, comportamiento controlante, expectativas no realistas, aislamiento, comportamiento acusante, crueldad, amenazas, cambio de humor y un papel rigido tanto para el hombre como para la mujer.

ELEMENTOS DE UNA RELACIÓN DISFUNCIONAL

Celos

La pareja violenta muchas veces cela todo y a todas aquellas personas en su vida, incluyendo su trabajo y los hijos que han tenido juntos. El hombre puede quejarse que nunca pasa suficiente tiempo con el y que nunca le da la suficiente atención. También podrá acusarle de darles mucha atención a otros miembros de la familia, a sus amistades, o a sus pasatiempos, actividades o trabajo. Muchas veces expresan sus celos tratando primeramente de razonar la situación, después haciendo "pucheros," discutiendo, amenazando o tratando de controlarla físicamente. Podrá seguirle o acecharle cuando salga, secretamente escuchar sus llamadas y abrir su correo sin su permiso. El no se sentirá cómodo con ninguna cosa que haga que no sea enfocado en él. Su pareja podrá ser capaz de tener una gran insistencia en sus esfuerzos por poseerla completamente. El tratara de bajarle el ánimo para finalmente lograr que pases menos tiempo con los demás. Su fin es que pares de hacer cosas que lo apartan sea aun cosas que para usted son importantes. Usted podrá abandonar el trabajo por hacer que su pareja se sienta más segura, pero nada de lo que haga será suficiente.

Control

La violencia doméstica genera control. Su pareja se siente fuera de control por dentro y el actúa con inseguridad tratando de controlarla. Quiere controlar lo que piensa y lo que siente, donde va, a quien ve, y lo que hace. Cuando pueda, hasta en las cosas más insignificantes, su pareja tratará de hacer que haga y vea las cosas a su manera. El le pedirá que se cambie el cabello, y el maquillaje, su manera de vestir, y después el hará que cambié todo esto nuevamente. El tratará de convencerla a no entender los asuntos financieros o políticos, y dejar que el mas bien se encargue en decidir como gastan el dinero familiar o como debes votar. Se enojará y atacará cuando trates de actuar independientemente o cuando quieras tomar decisiones propias, incluso cuando las decisiones no tienen nada que ver con el. En casos extremos, hasta el decidir lo que debes de comer para el almuerzo puedá que cause una discusión.

Expectativas No Realistas

Es probable que su pareja tenga expectativas no realistas sobre como debe ser la relación. Creerá que debe saber lo que el quiere y lo que el está pensando sin que el tenga que decir nada. El podrá asumir que usted cree y siente exactamente lo que el piensa y cree. Si el siente deseos de salir a comer un helado de chocolate, pensará que usted también lo debe desear. Creerá que usted sigue dándole la razón a su comportamiento sin importar cuan escandaloso o exigente sea.

Aislamiento

Su pareja querrá separarla de las demás personas y otras actividades que quite su atención. Exteriormente controlará sus relaciones con los demás, o secretamente y sutilmente tratará de sofocar su confianza y afecto por la gente que conoce. Mentirá sobre cosas que sus amistades o miembros de familia han dicho y hecho. Por ejemplo, como al decir que su mejor amiga le coquetea, o que el ha escuchado a su hermana decir que usted es una "estupida." Con el tiempo, sus comentarios negativos podrán causar desconfianza hasta en aquellas personas que son más cercanos. Cuando no pueda confiar en sus padres, hermanos, o sus mejores amigas, solo lo tendrás a el de apoyo, cumpliendo así lo que el quiere.

Cuando una mujer se expone a este comportamiento y cree que no puede salir empieza acomodarse. Aprende a tolerar el comportamiento, a creer, y adaptarse a los sentimientos que el a desarrollado. Su acomodación o amoldamiento permitirá que la relación continúe.

> Desde un principio de la relación, Danielle se molestó por algunos comportamientos que Mitch demostraba. La primera noche después de que se conocieron el empezó a importunarla a que tuvieran un compromiso exclusivo. Aunque ella trató de resistir su insistencia, eventualmente ella se doblegó, esperando que su promesa de exclusividad le ayudará a sentirse lo suficientemente segura para permitir que se relajara y disfrutara la relación. Tan pronto Danielle expresó su compromiso, Mitch empezó a quejarse que ella no pasaba suficiente tiempo con el. Hasta le molestaba que ella pasara tiempo con sus amigas o que le dedicara tiempo al trabajo o a los niños. Las discusiones con Mitch empezaron con pequeños debates, y al principio Danielle pudo sostener su punto de vista y rehusar de hacer le caso a sus quejas. Semanas pasaron y las peleas continuaron. Con el tiempo, Danielle empezó a cuestionarse. "Alomejor soy yo la del problema." "Tal ves no le estoy dando la suficiente atención." No importaba cuanto tiempo y energía Danielle le daba a la relación, sin embargo, Mitch nunca estuvo satisfecho. Las discusiones se agrandaron, se prologaron y se hicieron más difíciles. Pronto Mitch estaba acusando a Danielle de ser fría e incapaz de ser una buena amante. A medida que paso el tiempo, ella empezó a creer que el tenía la razón y que algo andaba mal en ella. Después del primer año en su relación, Danielle había bajado mucho su auto-estima y auto-valor. Se aislaba de su familia y de sus amigos, y aún había un cierto distanciamiento entre ella y sus niños. Danielle nunca más se sintió bien de si misma y

estaba constantemente buscando la aprobación de Mitch. Sus peleas ahora incluían a Mitch gritando, tomando, tirando cosas y culpándola por su perdida de control. Danielle se sentía mal y con temor, pero ella no se sintió lo suficientemente fuerte para arriesgar y terminar la relación. Ella cayó en la trampa de la violencia doméstica por aceptar y acomodarse a las exigencias irrazonables de Mitch.

A medida que la víctima de violencia doméstica se va ajustando y acomodando, empieza a experimentar muchos sentimientos dolorosos y síntomas de severa tensión. Estos son algunos de los sentimientos y comportamientos reportados por las víctimas de la violencia doméstica.

1. *Depresión*—sentimientos de tristeza, impotencia y desesperación. Testimonios dichos por las víctimas de violencia doméstica sobre la depresión:
   - "Yo no puedo recordar como se siente el ser feliz."
   - "Si yo me fuera, el estaría solo y no lo soportaría."
   - "No hay nada que pueda yo hacer."
   - "No hay salida. Yo hice mi cama; ahora me tengo que acostar en ella."
2. *Ansiedad*—sentimientos de ansiedad, incapacidad de enfrentar la situación, estar siempre al borde. Declaraciones dichas por las víctimas acerca de la ansiedad:
   - "Yo siento miedo todo el tiempo. No puedo dormir."
   - "Yo no puedo lidiar con la vida. Yo no puedo lidiar con nada."
   - "Yo no se porque soy así, ahora todo me incomoda."
3. *Disturbios al Dormir*—sin poder dormir, pesadillas, pavor nocturno. Esto es lo que siente al presenciar falta de sueño:
   - "Yo siempre estoy cansada. Nunca me siento descansada."
   - "No quiero cerrar mis ojos. Pasar por más pesadillas."
   - "¿Por qué no podré dormir como una persona normal?"
4. *Bajo Auto-Estima*—falta de auto-valor, una pobre auto-imagen, pensamientos de suicidio, sentimientos de impotencia. Así es como suena la falta de auto-valor:
   - "Yo no se porqué el se queda conmigo. Si no puedo hacer nada bien."

- "Estoy gorda y fea. Nadie mas me va a querer."
- "Quizás el y los niños estarán mejor sin mi."

5. *Expectativas No Realistas*—sentimientos que hacen creer que su pareja va a cambiar, que al cambiar su propio comportamiento, ella puede causar que el cambie:
   - "Cuando a el le den la promoción, el dejará de comportarse de esa manera."
   - "Yo se que lo puedo hacer feliz. Solo tengo que aprender hacer las cosas bien."
   - "El solo actúa así porque me quiere."

6. *Sentimientos de peligro*—sentimientos de peligro para si misma y para los niños. Estos son:
   - "No puedo llegar a la casa tarde; se pondrá furioso."
   - "Desearía irme, pero si el no llegara a encontrarme me iría peor."
   - "Me quitara los niños si yo trato de irme."

7. *Trastorno al comer*—hartazgo del comer, purgarse, o el comer en exceso etc. Esto el lo que pasa cuando sufres trastorno al comer:
   - Usted come aun cuando no tiene hambre porque come para alimentar su corazón y no su estómago.
   - Empieza comiendo solo una galleta; de repente se da cuenta que se ha comido toda la caja.
   - Comes demás y resultas vomitando la comida metiendose el dedo a la boca. Aun se siente vacía, enferma y quieres comer otra vez.

CICLO DE VIOLENCIA

En una relación abusiva hay un ciclo de violencia. Inicialmente, la relación no incluye violencia. Una de las razones que mantiene muchas víctimas con el ofensor es que la violencia ocurre despacio y en períodos largos. El ciclo es seductivo (es tentador) y intensificante (empeorándose con el tiempo). Al principio es difícil ver que el comportamiento de su pareja pueda causar daño y que vaya a ser peligroso. El comportamiento se vuelve mas y mas violento a medida que pasa el tiempo. Muchas veces empieza lentamente con solo pucheros, discusiones y después vienen los gritos, las culpas, los golpes a las paredes, empujos, y finalmente agresión física. ! A la hora que se dan cuenta que la relación es violenta, ya se ha acostumbrado al abuso.

Margurite estaba emocionada cuando su vecino empezó a llamarle la atención. El era muy atractivo, encantador, y tenía un buen trabajo. Sus primeras citas fueron románticas y emocionantes. En una semana, Fernando empezó a presionarla a que se comprometieran. La relación parecía perfecta al principio. Después lentamente, Margurite notó que Fernando se estaba volviendo posesivo y exigente. Ella trató de contarle sus preocupaciones y el aparentemente estuvo de acuerdo entrando en razón y luego apartándose. Pero en vez de tener las presiones cotidianas de una relación, el empezó a molestarla por asuntos menores. Ella no quería empeorar la relación, por eso hizo todo lo posible de hacerlo sentir cómodo. Gradualmente, Margurite notó que ella y Fernando estaban discutiendo con más frecuencia. Sin embargo, cuando no estaban en desacuerdo, todo estaba a la maravilla. Meses pasaron y Margurite pudo ver que Fernando tenía un temperamento fuerte. Por haber llegado tarde a una cita con el, se enojo, le gritó y le pegó mandándola hacia la pared con un puño. Su enojo fue tan explosivo que atemorizó a Margurite haciendola llorar. Fernando rápidamente se calmó y empezó a consolarla. Margurite pensó que su perdida de control era de solo una vez. Ella no pudo ver que ese incidente era solo el principio del ciclo de violencia.

Reconocer que la relación es abusiva es a veces difícil porque la pareja no se la pasa enojado o se violenta todo el tiempo. Toda relación tiene su propio patrón de altos y bajos. En algunas relaciones, la violencia explosiva ocurre diariamente o semanalmente. En otros, la violencia no ocurre con frecuencia. Con algunas parejas, años pueden pasar entre una y otra explosión de violencia. Cuando la violencia no es frecuente hace que sea mas difícil para que la víctima se libere de la relación; durante cada período de calma, ella cree que el ciclo ha finalizado.

A medida que el ofensor va por el ciclo de violencia, su comportamiento cambia. Estos cambios en su comportamiento pueden confundirla. El ciclo empieza con la acumulación de tensión en la relación. Puede empezar simplemente como un sentimiento de tensión o inconformidad cuando esta con su pareja. Después hay un período de crítica, culpa, gritos, e intimidación. Nada de lo que haga esta bien

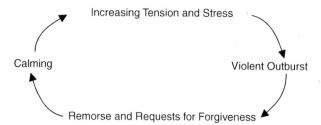

y cualquier cosa que haga "mal" es por su culpa. Entre mas trate de corregir lo que hizo mal, mas será culpada. La tensión continúa aumentándose hasta que haya una explosión.

Durante la etapa violenta del ciclo, algún tipo de violencia física tiende a ocurrir. El ofensor puede tener un momento de furia y empezar a tirar o romper cosas, pegarle a la pared, empujar, patear o golpear. Es en este momento que empieza a sentir temor. A veces otros escuchan la explosión de la violencia y llaman a la policía. Durante las explosiones de violencia puedes pensar en irse, salirse de la relación. Se podrá dar cuenta que usted no merece ese castigo, que usted no tiene que vivir bajo ese tipo de tensión. Desarrollará un plan para salirse definitivamente o temporalmente.

Después de la explosión, sin embargo, su pareja expresará pena y remordimiento por lo ocurrido. El aparentemente llegará a entender lo que hizo y prometerá nunca ser violento con usted otra vez. Su petición de ser perdonado revive el sueño que las cosas cambiaran, que la relación va mejorar. Promesas y aseguranzas de amor causan que no termine con la relación. Derepente, tiene otra vez la esperanza. En el ciclo de violencia, la etapa del perdón va a la mano con la etapa de la luna de miel. De cualquier manera, sin ayuda, intervención o alguna consecuencia, la luna de miel sólo durará un corto tiempo. Eventualmente, la tensión empezará ha aumentar y el ciclo se repetirá.

Cuando usted se encuentre fuera de control, la tensión precipita el ciclo de la violencia doméstica. La tensión proviene por condiciones del hogar o de la relación, pero la tensión también se precipita por otras situaciones que pueda ocurrir en la vida de su pareja, tales como su trabajo, presiones económicas o presiones internas que trae consigo mismo del pasado o traumas que no haya resuelto. Las reacciones de su pareja, son similares a las suyas, porque envuelve el comportamiento aprendido en el pasado. Si su pareja no ha tenido la oportunidad de aprender maneras constructivas de expresar su frustración, la violencia resultara la manera más natural de desaguar el enojo.

El ciclo de violencia es predicible y continuará ocurriendo por más que intentes pararlo. Todos en su familia tendrá que participar si desean romper el ciclo de violencia. El primer paso requiere reconocer que no eres culpable, y que no podrás controlar, el comportamiento de su pareja. Si tienen niños, vas a querer ser un ejemplo para ellos. Vas a querer reducir las veces que tengan que aprender lecciones equivocadas, al trazar límites o barreras hacia comportamientos destructivos o no saludables. Querrás que tus niños entiendan lo que pueden y lo que no pueden controlar. Le tendrás que enseñar las mismas lecciones que necesitas aprender, por ejemplo, que uno no es la causa, el control ni la cura en el comportamiento violento de los demás.

En el capítulo tres, hablaremos más sobre los efectos de la violencia doméstica en los niños y como se les puede enseñar a evitar relaciones enfermizas. Viviendo en medio de la violencia doméstica eventualmente destruye su auto-estima, auto-valor y su auto-confianza. Si eres constantemente criticado, culpado, intimidado, o físicamente irrespetado, por medio de empujos, patadas, golpes, violación sexual, eventualmente llegaras a creer que algo en usted o algo que ha hecho causó el abuso, por resultado su auto-estima y auto-valor decae al ver lo que esta sucediendo.

Mientras el ciclo de violencia y el comportamiento de su pareja este fuera de control, es probable que empieces a perder seguridad en la habilidad de manejar la propia vida. A medida que empieces a sentir la incapacidad de controlar la violencia, también podrás empezar a cuestionar la habilidad de controlar otros aspectos de la vida. El sentir que sus decisiones y acciones son constantemente criticadas y cuestionadas, provoca que uno llegue a dudar de si misma. También empezarás a perder seguridad en la habilidad de tomar decisiones en cuanto a la vestimenta, como gastas el dinero, como crías los niños, como deberías ser con sus amistades y otros familiares o como relacionarse en el trabajo.

La perdida de auto-estima, auto-valor, y seguridad en si misma hace que sea difícil que veas claramente su capacidad de terminar la relación y a la vez sobrevivir. Con baja auto-estima y baja auto-valor empezaras a cuestionar si alguna otra persona llegara amarla, y si alguna vez podrás obtener una relación. El pensar que estarás sola por toda una vida podrá ser muy triste y doloroso de confrontar. Creerás que el quedarse en una relación enfermiza es mejor que no tener una relación.

El perder la seguridad en si misma, especialmente si se extiende hacia el trabajo o su profesión, también apoyará a que se quede en una relación enfermiza. Podrás sentir que es muy difícil tomar las decisiones necesarias para dejar la relación. Probablemente encontraras que por más que deseas dejar la relación, tendrás dificultad pagando las cuentas y tendrás que pensar a donde vivir y como cuidar a los niños. Muchas veces optan por quedarse en la relación simplemente por que no crees tener otra opción.

Maria era una fisioterapista exitosa, dueña de su propio negocio, cuando conoció a Ricardo, un paciente con un serio problema en la rodilla. Aunque era casado, Ricardo y Maria eventualmente se involucraron en una relación íntima; dos años después, el dejo a su esposa. Maria nunca pensó que Ricardo era posesivo; al contrario ella interpretaba sus constante críticas como su manera de ayudarla a crecer, y sus demandas como un reflejó de cuanto la necesitaba y la quería. Al paso de los meses, Maria le puso más energía y devoción en contentar a Ricardo y en aliviar sus necesidades, deseos, y preocupaciones sobre el trabajo, los niños, su problemas, y su dolor. Hasta que un día Ricardo empezó a despertar a Maria a la media noche para que escuchar a sus preocupaciones y para que le diera masajes en la pierna. Por más que esto le molestaba, ella puso su resentimiento a un lado y excusó su comportamiento. Muchos años después que empezaran la relación, Maria desarrolló una enfermedad peligrosa. Su negoció no dio resultado porque ella no pudo trabajar con regularidad. Sus amistades y familiares también se apartaron, expresándole a Maria con mucha delicadeza que Ricardo los hacia sentir incómodos. Cuando Maria estuvo hospitalizada con cáncer del seno, una trabajadora social la fue a visitar y trato de ayudarle a que viera cuan consumida estaba por la relación. Aunque Ricardo no fue físicamente abusivo con ella, sus constantes críticas y demandas habían destruido su seguridad. Ahora el cáncer que traia Maria decayó la poco auto-estima que le quedaba. Ella se sintió completamente dependiente de Ricardo económicamente y emocionalmente. Ella no podía imaginar su existencia sin el. Cualquier comportamiento que Ricardo fuera a demostrar en un futuro, Maria no podría contemplar la idea de dejarlo.

El abuso emocional o verbal tiene como intención destruir sus sentimientos positivos para que no puedas lograr dejar la relación. En el interior de un ofensor, existe una persona insegura de si misma y que se siente inferior ante los demás. El se siente atemorizado y bombardeado cuando estas fuerte y feliz consigo misma; por ende razón, es que el ataca esas cualidades. A medida que usted se sienta mal de si misma, su pareja se siente mas fuerte, pero a la vez se enoja porque el cree no poderla respetar. Estas reacciones trabajan juntas en un ciclo vicioso que contribuyen a la violencia.

Quizás encuentres que los valores o creencias aprendidas en la niñez sobre el matrimonio, la lealtad, y el compromiso estén en conflicto con su deseo o necesidad de dejar la relación. Las reacciones de otros miembros de la familia y sus creencias religiosas puedan causar que pienses que el dejar la relación no es una opción. Valores familiares o religiosos son factores importantes al tomar una decisión sobre la relación, y es apropiado que todos estos factores sean considerados. Sin embargo, es importante no utilizar un sistema de valores idealizados para evadir el confrontar la responsabilidad que tienes hacia si misma de permanecer fuera de peligro.

Si estas en una relación con un ofensor, es esencial que reconozcas que nada de lo que hagas, incluyendo el sacrificar su seguridad y su valor propio, cambiará la situación. La violencia podrá terminar solo si su pareja, por si mismo, reconoce el problema y decide por sus propios motivos buscar ayuda.

Capítulo 3

Los Efectos de la Violencia Doméstica en los Niños

COMO LOS NIÑOS SE DESARROLLAN BAJO TENSIÓN

En el curso del desarrollo infantil, la energía biológica de cada niño se mueve con naturalidad empezando desde sus primeras tareas de supervivencia hacia pasos más complejos y sofisticados. Niños en la infancia, por ejemplo, aprenden a regular su habilidad para comer y dormir en un patrón rutinario. Ellos gradualmente se empiezan a ver a si mismo como un objeto interesante y a la vez empiezan a relacionarse con sus alrededores y con aquellos que los rodean. Si niños crecen en un medio ambiente seguro, su desarrollo se desenvuelve con naturalidad. Ellos se sienten seguros al ser móvil, sentarse, gatear, caminar, y finalmente correr. Ellos aprenden a comunicar y eventualmente separarse de la protección de sus padres o de aquellos que lo cuidan. En el intento de hacer un lugar para ellos en el mundo logran examinar sus fuerzas y habilidades.

Niños en la infancia que crecen bajo tensión y confusión no pueden enfocarse en su desarrollo en una manera normal. La mayoría de su energía es utilizada para tratar de entender, lidiar con y protegerse de eventos atemorizantes que le rodean. El ajustarse al mundo puede atrazar, distorcionar, e interrumpir el curso natural del desarollo.

Infancia

Como ha sido mencionado, la violencia doméstica tiene un efecto dramático sobre los niños. Esto puede empezar cuando la criatura esta en el vientre. Más del 50 porciento de las mujeres embarazadas que están en una relación abusiva son golpeadas aun cuando están embarazadas.

Aunque el niño nazca saludable, niños criados en medio de la violencia doméstica empiezan a vivir con riesgos físicos, mentales, emocionales y espirituales. Durante la infancia, al trazar un lazo con la madre, estos niños pueden experimentar dificultades. Ella podrá distanciarse de sus hijos para que ellos no tengan que afrentar el peligro o al contrario pueda tratar de mantener sus hijos muy cerca de ella para protegerse a si misma de la violencia. La madre podrá utilizar sus hijos como una coraza, creyendo que ella no será abusada si ella toma en sus brazos a su niño. Desafortunadamente, ya que empiece el abuso físico, la mayoría de las madres encuentran que sus criaturas no les provee la protección y, que aun, sus acciones ponen en riesgo a sus hijos.

En una escena de violencia doméstica los otros riesgos que sufren los niños incluyen interrupciones en el horario de comer y dormir, la reducción del afecto constante, el riesgar que el niño sea lastimado al sacudirlos, dejarlos caer, pegarles con un objeto, o a propósito lastimarlos. Todos estos riesgos son una amenaza hacia el desarrollo natural de un niño.

La Edad Preescolar

Niños en la edad preescolar llevan los efectos de la violencia doméstica a todas las áreas de su vida. Ellos podrán sufrir disturbios al dormir pueden experimentar pesadillas que los despiertan gritando; quedando absolutamente aterrorizados por sus sueños. Comportamientos regresivos tales como el chuparse el dedo, el estar constantemente apegado, o cuando se orina en la cama después de haber sido entrenado a orinar en la taza pueden ser causas de la confusión e inseguridad.

Durante los años pre-escolares, niños internalizan los comportamientos observados, empezando que esto efectúa el proceso del aprendizaje. Esta etapa del desarrollo mental permite que los niños crean que ellos son el centro del mundo, y por ende, los responsables de todo; esto provoca que ellos se sientan culpables por la violencia. Constante con su desarrollo natural, los niños tambien llegan a identificarse con el pariente del mismo sexo. Muchas veces, el niño trata de modelar el ejemplo del hombre en la familia (usualmente el agresor) mientras la niña aprende a modelar el papel de la mujer (usualmente la victima).

Los Años Elementarios

Cuando Juan de nueve años y Maria de diez años llegaron al la casa de refugio, eran niños muy difíciles de tratar. Sufrian dificultades al mantener la concentración y cuando se enojaban o se frustraban, Juan se ponía violento y Maria lo apoyaba. Los otros niños le tenían miedo. Cuando un ayudante del refugio trato de corregir su comportamiento trazándole limites y consecuencias, su madre trato de rescatarlos, como ella antes hacia con el padre de los niños. La madre inicialmente culpaba al refugio y a los otros niños por ser una mala influencia. Ella decía que el comportamiento de los niños era peor en el refugio de lo que era en la casa. Ella no se daba cuenta que el refugio, los hacia sentir más seguros de revelar su temor y enojo.

Durante los años escolares, el comportamiento de los niños muchas veces continua siendo diferente al de las niñas. Esto se basa mas que todo en el pariente con quien el niño se llega a identificar que suele ser el pariente de su mismo sexo. Su comportamiento se llama género específico; que significa que el niño generalmente demuestra diferentes actitudes y comportamientos que al de las niñas. Niños muchas veces se comportan mal o externalizan la tensión que están viviendo. Mientras las niñas, tienden a internalizar su dolor y tensión. Esto significa que los niños que frecuentemente se involucran en comportamientos agresivos han vivido bajo la violencia doméstica, incluyendo peleas, desobediencia en la casa y en la escuela, y la destrucción de propiedad. Mientras las niñas son más propensas a sufrir depresión, ansiedad, y aislarse de los demás. Por ejemplo, estos niños empiezan a quejarse del dolor físico, de dolor de estomago o dolores de cabeza. Estos papeles género específicos, sin embargo, no son tan rígidos que tenga que excluir la posibilidad que unos de los sexos no vaya a exhibir algunos de esos comportamientos que comúnmente se ven en el sexo opuesto. En otras palabras, las niñas pueden llegar a comportasen mal y los niños pueden sufrir dolor de estomago. Desafortunadamente, por su comportamiento agresivo, el niño varón muchas veces atrae la mayor parte de la atención, dejando a que la niña, que también sufre, sea ignorada.

Problemas en la escuela empiezan a aumentar durante este tiempo. Estos niños pueden que estén tan preocupados por lo que esta pasando en casa que ellos no puedan concentrasen en el aprendizaje. El desarrollo social también se empieza afectar cuando el niño, quien no ha aprendido métodos constructivos de resolver conflictos, se confunde al ser confrontados por parámetros interpersonales. Pueda que el niño que se de mas o menos hacia las amistades, tenga dificultades al saber como relajarse con la fluidez natural de una relación. Algunos niños, al contrario, podrán escapar de sus problemas enfocándose intensamente en el estudio, tanto en lo académico como en lo social.

Interferencia Académica

El desarrollo escolar puede ser dramáticamente afectado por la violencia doméstica en un número de maneras específicas:

1. El niño falta a la escuela por quedarse en la casa ha proteger a la mama.
2. El niño no entrega sus tareas a tiempo por su inhabilidad de concentración en la casa, especialmente durante las etapas de la violencia donde la tensión va aumentando y hay una explosión.
3. Los niños se podrán quedar dormidos en la clase porque temen quedarse dormidos en casa. Muchas veces esto sucede por miedo a que su madre sea lastimada mientras dormian. Esto, mas las pesadillas, pueden causar que el niño este cansado o se quede dormido en la clase. Estos problemas pueden resultar en una pérdida de progreso académico, bajas calificaciones, baja auto-estima, y más problemas en la casa.

Interferencia Social

Niños de familias violentas tienen dificultad al traer amigos a la casa. Ellos no han aprendido como las interacciones sociales funcionan, experimentan problemas al establecer confianza en las relaciones y tienen dificultad reconociendo situaciones amenazantes. Algunos niños llegan a ser "parentificados"; eso significa que ellos llegan a crecer muy rápido tratando de asumir el papel de adulto o pariente. Muchas veces asumen este papel en el intento de cuidar al pariente que esta siendo abusado o para proteger a sus hermanos menores. Estos niños están especialmente a riesgo de ser lastimados por un incidente de violencia, de correr peligro en situaciones que no reconoce ser peligrosas, y a veces llegan hasta intentar el suicidio.

Adolescentes

Marcos pasaba mucho tiempo solo con su padre arreglando la casa. Cuando su hermana mayor, Riley, le expreso su frustración por no proteger a su madre de los asaltos de su padre, Marcos explico que el temía interferir por miedo de que fuera a pegarle cuando el y su padre estuvieran solos. Tanto Marcos como Riley les confiaron a sus amistades que ellos no querían tener hijos; ellos no querían tener un niño que temiera como ellos temen a su padre.

Los años de la adolescencia es una etapa cuando los niños buscan independizarse. Adolescentes que han sido expuestos a la violencia doméstica, sin embargo, podrán no tener la habilidad de manejar esta fase de su vida exitosamente por la disrupción de su desarrollo a tan temprana edad. El adolescente que esta siendo retado por la vida en este momento podrá utilizar un número de respuestas.

El hecho que las cosas en casa estén tan difíciles, el adolescente que ha vivido con violencia doméstica podrá conseguir una familia substituta (pandillas o grupos que abusan las drogas o el alcohol, etc.) donde se sientan aceptados. Estas amistades pueden conducirlos a comportamientos agresivos, antisociales, o criminales y aun pueden experimentar más dificultades en ajustarse a la casa o la escuela. Aunque una familia substituta no fuese hallada, comportamientos antisociales pueden ocurrir (robar, abuso de substancias, disturbios en la escuela) como una manera de atraer atención a si mismos. Atención negativa es mejor que no recibir atención alguna. El suicidio es también una preocupación en algunos de estos casos.

Basado en las experiencias que los adolescentes han tenido con sus familias, ellos son vulnerables al tener relaciones abusivas. Violencia en una relación parece ser algo normal, algunos adolescentes hasta creen que una relación abusiva es mejor que no tener relación alguna. La violación en una cita, que con frecuencia no es reportada, llega a ser un problema comúnmente visto en los adolescentes.

Adolescentes que actúan con violencia usualmente creen que la violencia es una forma apropiada de resolver el conflicto y una manera de obtener respeto y control. Algunos creen que la violencia puede ser explicada si hay una razón o excusa, tal como el beber o alguna otra provocación.

Los Efectos Emocionales de la Violencia en los Niños

Niños que son testigos de la violencia doméstica pueden experimentar todas las mismas emociones dolorosas y síntomas de tensión sentidas por la victima. Los niños pueden sufrir depresión, ansiedad o problemas al dormir, o hasta pueden llegar a desarrollar sentimientos de inferioridad. Muchos niños sienten impotencia y sin la esperanza hacia el futuro, mientras otros sienten enojo y furia. Algunos niños generalizan sus experiencias en la casa y empiezan a ver o sentir peligro en todo lugar. Ellos llegan a aislarsen, a sospechar, o aun sentir paranoia hacia la gente. Niños pueden desarrollar problemas con la alimentación, empiezan a revelarsen sexualmente, o empiezan a usar drogas o alcohol para escapar el temor y dolor que sienten como resultado de la violencia familiar.

Sus hijos quieren y necesitan ser protegidos de la violencia y requieren de un adulto fuerte y saludable que se pueda cuidar a si misma y a ellos. Si es necesario, hasta estar dispuesta a dejar la relación.

La mala noticia para los niños que crecen en un hogar violento es que ellos pueden sufrir problemas emocionales, físicos, académicos, y sociales. La buena noticia es que los niños son increíblemente resistentes. Con la ayuda apropiada, los niños pueden recuperarse de los efectos de la violencia doméstica y aprender mejores maneras de relacionarse a otros.

Capítulo 4

El Ofensor

Chan era caballeroso e inteligente. El mantenia un trabajo estable con un buen ingreso económico y solo criaba a su hijo. Maureen creyó que finalmente había conseguido el hombre de sus sueños. La primera semana toda parecía perfecto. Pero luego las quejas comenzaron cuando. Chan empezo a sentirse rechazado. Chan se que-jaba que Maureen no pasaba suficiente tiempo con el y ni le prestaba atención. El no confiaba en ella, la presionaba por un compromiso estable, queriendo trazar la fecha de la boda. Meses despues Maureen en varias ocasiones trato de romper la relación. Las quejas constantes de Chan la estaban agotando. El había comenzado a decirle necedades. Atacando su personalidad, haciéndola sentir culpable e inferior. Cuando intentaba romper la relación, Chan regresaba pidiendo perdón y prometiendo cambiar. Paso un año y los argumentos se hicieron más fuertes, largos, y destructivos. Aun cuando Chan buscaba reestablecer la relación, Maureen accedía. "Yo se que pelear no es bueno" ella dijo, "pero solo quiero ayudar a que Chan se sienta mas seguro. No es como si nuestra relación sea en verdad violenta, después de todo no es que el me pegara o algo por el estilo."

Muchas cosas incentivaban a que Maureen siguiera en la relación a pesar de los problemas que Chan tenía con su inseguridad y enojo. Primeramente ella estaba muy atraída a el. Su cargo en el trabajo y su apariencia de ser buen padre la incentivo a seguir en la relación. Mas que todo, Maureen estaba impresionada por su determinación y su persistencia de estar con ella. Ella pensaba, "el me ama demasiado. A pesar de todo lo que soporta el sigue regresando conmigo."

Maureen no se consideraba una victima de violencia doméstica. Por mas que Chan no hubiese utilizado la violencia física, las peleas entre los dos estaban afectando su auto-estima. Si la relación continuara, probablemente la frecuencia e intensidad de las peleas, hubíeran resultado en violencia física.

No existe característica o razón alguna en el ofensor que explique porque el hace lo que hace. No se puede identificar al ofensor cuando se conoce. El se ve como cualquier otra persona, puede ser su amigo, vecino, doctor, hermano o hasta usted mismo.

El ciclo de la violencia doméstica es íntergenérico; en la mayor parte de los casos, es un patrón de comportamiento violento que se aprende en casa. Los ofensores han aprendido que por medio de las amenazas, intimidación, y la violencia ellos pueden obtener el control de sus hogares. Las lecciones de la violencia doméstica se aprenden por medio de personas expuestas, experiencias y algunos familiares. Solamente algunos familiares selectos, como la madre y sus hijas, son lastimadas. En otras familias, los hijos pueden ser duramente criticados, degradados, humillados, pateados, golpeados o empujados. En algunas familias puede que sea los abuelos contra los niños; esto es el comienzo de un riesgo hacia el abuso en si mismo.

En el interior de cada ofensor hay un individuo frágil e inseguro, bombardeado por sentimientos de inferioridad, ansiedad, depresión, y furia reprimida. Estos poderosos sentimientos hacen que el ofensor en su diario vivir se sienta impotente. Como la victima, el ofensor se siente confuso y atemorizado, sin la capacidad de considerar una variedad de opciones. Cuando esta molesto el reacciona impulsivamente, acertándose de una manera agresiva para tratar de controlar su medio ambiente y la gente que le rodea. Sin ninguna intervención, de esta manera el comportamiento del ofensor continuara y empeorara.

El ofensor se puede encontrar en cualquier sociedad económica, racial, étnica, educativo y entre diversas edades. Aunque la mujer puede ser violenta, la mayoría de los ofensores son hombres. Algunos ofensores son fáciles de reconocer porque siempre parecen estar enojados y son predecibles. Pero otros pueden parecer perfectamente "normales" en su comportamiento diario, solo saliendo a relucir en algunas circunstancias estresantes. No importa cual sea el estilo del ofensor, todos son igualmente peligrosos.

Estos son algunas de las características en el comportamiento de los ofensores:

- En el comienzo de toda relación tiende haber una presión inmediata para hacer planes hacia el futuro. Aunque no haya llegado a una solidez estable en la relación.

- A medida que la relación continua, el puede demostrar falta de control sobre sus impulsos y su temperamento y enojo son impredecibles.
- El exceso de celos es expresado y acusaciones son hechos contra usted. El intenta controlar sus actividades y su contacto con otras personas. El invade su privacidad, abre su correo, escucha sus mensajes telefónicos, y aun esculca su propiedad privada.
- El trata de aislarla de su familia y amistades, reclamando que su compañía debería satisfacerla totalmente.

El ofensor tiene una variedad de mecanismos de defensas mentales y emocionales que lo ayudan a justificar su comportamiento. El culpa a otros por sus fracasos y problemas, usando racionalización, minimización, proyección, y negación para explicar sus acciones y evadir responsabilidad de su comportamiento. Mientras el ofensor pueda mantener la creencia que su comportamiento violento es justificable y excusable, el no podrá efectuar ningún cambio en su acciones.

- El mantiene un papel rígido hacia el hombre y la mujer y puede ser forzoso durante el sexo.
- El es físicamente y verbalmente cruel hacia los niños, animales y hacia usted.
- El usualmente abusa alcohol y otras substancias.

Usted podrá ver otros comportamientos que son peligrosos; sin embargo, los comportamientos que se han presentado son los mas comunes.

Hombres que son abusivos muchas veces consideran a su pareja y a sus hijos como su propiedad, esperando que ellos satisfagan ciertos papeles y se comporten en ciertas maneras específicas. El ofensor se molesta cuando gente extraña, incluyendo familia, amigos, o las autoridades como la policía o la corte interfieren. El ofensor cree que esta en su derecho de controlar a la familia, trazar expectativas, e imponer la disciplina como el la ve necesaria, si intervención de alguien afuera. Las creencias de muchos de los ofensores son reforzadas cuando la victima, vecinos, o amistades llaman a las autoridades y las autoridades fallan en tomar acción. Después de algunos incidentes donde las autoridades se involucran y ninguna consecuencia es recibida, el ofensor podrá empezar a sentir apoyo de las autoridades.

Cual sea la causa de la agresión, sea genético, aprendido, o relacionado al abuso de substancias, el cambio no se dará acabo hasta que el ofensor experimente consecuencias serias por su comportamiento. El comportamiento violento es generalmente aprendido a muy temprana edad y es, por lo tanto, asociado con emociones intensas y primitivas, que el ofensor honestamente se llega a sentir fuera de control. Los siguientes comentarios fueron escuchados en un grupo de ofensores:

- "Por culpa de esa perra. Yo le di todo, pero nada de eso fue suficiente. Ella siempre quiso más y me seguía reclamando. Yo no le hubiera pegado si ella no me hubiera empujado."
- "Por culpa de la policía. Ellos salieron y ni me escucharon. Ellos tomaron su lado. Ellos habían venido muchas veces antes y nunca paso nada."
- "Si yo hubiera tenido el dinero para contratar un abogado no me hubieran condenado. El ofensor público no le importa. De todas formas todos le creen a la mujer. ¿Pero y mis derechos que?"

Para que el cambio ocurra, el ofensor deberá tener un poco de introspección sobre sus comportamientos inapropiados. El deberá ser capaz de entender que en vez de lograr la seguridad, amor, y la atención que necesitaba, el ser posesivo, los celos, y la violencia destruyo a sus seres queridos y los condujo a tener resentimiento, rechazo, y hasta odio. En la mayoría de los casos, el cambio solo ocurre cuando el ofensor se da cuenta que su comportamiento abusivo le da mas perdidas que ganancias.

Es posible que un evento natural y aun traumático, tales como una enfermedad en la familia, un accidente, o el fallecimiento de un ser querido sea necesario para que tome concienca, pueda reflexionar y lo motive a que reevalué su comportamiento. Otras consecuencias, tales como la perdida de su esposa e hijos, el ser arrestado, o la causa de un daño irrevocable en alguien quien el estima, puede influenciar el esfuerzo a que cambie. Desdichadamente, sin consecuencias naturales, emocionales, o legales el ofensor no tendrá razón para cambiar.

Muchos ofensores encuentran que sus problemas y actitudes se agrandan a resultado del abuso de substancias. Existe una relación fuerte entre el abuso de las drogas o el alcohol y la violencia doméstica. Miembros de la familia pueden reportar que la violencia ocurre solo cuando el ofensor esta tomando o usando drogas, o cuando el esta sufriendo la tensión de su desintoxicación. Sin embargo, es importante reconocer, que el abuso del alcohol y las drogas no causan el comportamiento abusivo. Ellos solo son racionalizaciones. Asuntos sobre el abuso de substancias y dependencia química deberán ser tratados para que el cambio sea significante y duradero. El ofensor no puede evaluar su comportamiento o traer cambio a su vida sin que el este limpio y sobrio por un periodo de tiempo significativo. El participar en un programa de drogas y alcohol y la afiliación a un grupo de Alcohólicos Anónimos (AA) o Narcóticos Anónimos (NA) son programas esenciales para sobrepasar el comportamiento violento.

Capítulo 5

Lo Que Puedes Hacer

Una relación violenta es un peligro para su sobreviviencia física, mental, emocional y espiritual. Aunque usted ame a su pareja, usted debe de entender que su amor no puede cambiar, controlar, o curar el comportamiento violento. Usted merece vivir libre de la amenaza a la violencia.

Muchas victimas de violencia doméstica permanecen con el ofensor por su baja auto-estima y falta de auto-valor. En otras palabras, algunas victimas pueden llegar a amar al ofensor mas de lo que se aman a si mismas. Ellas pueden llegar a creer que el es mas importante, que su vida es mas valiosa, y que sus necesidades deben de ser cumplidas. Esta perspectiva no es saludable y es muy peligrosa. En una relación saludable, la pareja llega a quererse a si mismo tanto como se llega a querersen mutuamente.

Amarse a si misma no significa que uno sea egoísta, egocéntrico, o despreocupado. Simplemente significa que su seguridad, felicidad, y bienestar merece atención. El otro significado es el poder ejercer el derecho de vivir libre de la violencia que su pareja impuso debido sus sentimientos de inseguridad y dolor.

Muchas de las parejas que experimentan conflicto matrimonial utilizan conserjería familiar o conyugal para resolver sus diferencias. Parejas que experimentan violencia como parte del conflicto matrimonial podrán también creer que ellos podrán recibir ayuda por medio de consejería. Desdichadamente, la consejería de familias y entre parejas no se ha encontrado ser útil para familias donde hay violencia. En la consejería conyugal y familiar, la relación es vista como el enfoque, y la violencia es vista tan solo como un síntoma. En muchas ocasiones durante la conserjería, es difícil que la persona abusada sea abierta y honesta en la presencia del ofensor. Ella podrá temer que después de la sesión, el ofensor pueda atacar con violencia por los hechos revelados durante la sesión. También, el hecho que la consejería es dirigida a mantener la relación, es probable que a la mujer la hagan en parte responsable por la violencia. El creer que la victima es responsable por el abuso, pueda reenforzar al ofensor que su comportamiento es razonable y aceptable. Aunque la consejería conyugal pueda ser de algún valor y sea que los dos individuos seriamente esten trabajando en la relación, es probable que pueda ser útil solo después de haber tratado otros tipos de terapias. Otras terapias puede traer cambios necesarios, hacia el concepto de poder y el control, tanto en la victima como en el ofensor.

Los ofensores pueden beneficiar de terapia individual, pero aun la terapia individual tiene sus limitaciones. En la terapia individual, se le permite al ofensor enfocarse en como manejar su enojo, mientras la raíz fundamental de su problema con el enojo y la agresión, tales como el aprendizaje defectuoso y asuntos sobre el origen familiar, son minimizadas o ignoradas. En la terapia individual, el ofensor tiene la oportunidad de manipular y moldear el punto de vista del terapista sobre su vida familiar. Sin chequear con los demás miembros de la familia, el terapista no tiene manera alguna de saber si el ofensor honestamente esta cambiando su comportamiento.

La terapia individual puede ser una influencia importante en la recuperación de la violencia doméstica, pero para ser efectivo debe ser visto como una pequeña parte de un gran sistema. La terapia individual, tanto para el ofensor como para la victima, debe siempre incluir un resumen detallado de sus antecedentes familiares y relacionales.

Un completo procedimiento para el ofensor de violencia doméstica deberá incluir los siguientes componentes:

1. El ofensor debe tomar la responsabilidad civil y criminal
2. Durante el curso de tratamiento para el ofensors, deben proveer protección y apoyo hacia la mujer y sus hijos
3. El tratamiento de abuso de substancias y dependencia química, incluyendo la afiliación a AA o NA
4. La terapia en grupo para el ofensor (En la terapia en grupo, el ofensor es confrontado por otros como el, otros con quien el se identifica y reconoce todas las maneras que el trata de evadir el aceptar responsabilidad por su comportamiento. La confrontación en grupo tiene el poder de traspasar las defensas emocionales y la negación, de cierta manera que ni individuos, tales como los familiares, amistades, o el terapista mismo ha podido lograr.)
5. La terapia en grupo para la victima (En la terapia en grupo, la victima es dada el apoyo y la guía practica para protegerse a si

misma y a sus hijos. Al romper su aislamiento ella tiene la oportunidad de mirar las percepciones y creencias destructivas que han sido desarrolladas como resultado de la influencia que tiene el ofensor sobre la victima.)

6. La terapia para los niños (En la terapia en grupo, los niños son asegurados que la violencia en casa no es su culpa. Miembros de la familia comparten el temor, dolor, y furia que resulta de la violencia, y cada niño aprende que su familia no es la única familia que experimentan dificultades. Los niños también son educados en como manejar sus propias inseguridades, enojo y sobre todo como mantenerse seguros de la violencia en casa.)

7. Terapia individual para el ofensor (En la terapia individual, el ofensor puede explorar las raíces de su comportamiento violento. El puede examinar la crisis o el trauma de su niñez que puedan haber causado enojo, puede llegar a entender sus percepciones, y hasta puede llegar a identificar esos comportamientos aprendidos. Esto lo ayudara a construir seguridad en si mismo y a desarrollar cierta herramientas que le ayude a manejar su comportamiento destructivo.)

8. Terapia individual para la victima (En la terapia individual, la victima puede resolver su crisis y trauma del pasado, aprender nuevos patrones de comportamientos, y reconstruir su auto-estima y su auto-valor.)

9. La terapia de niños (En la terapia individual, los niños de familias violentas puede expresar sus sentimientos por medio del juego, arte, movimiento, y la comunicación. La terapia permite que los niños resuelvan sus temores y preocupaciones, desarrollen herramientas para saber como controlar su enojo, y aprendan métodos de auto-protección. La terapista de los niños puede ayudar a que entiendan que la violencia entre adultos no es culpa de ellos y, a la vez, logre animarlos a que se sientan más seguros.)

Cuando la terapia no funciona o no es la respuesta, debes hallar otras soluciones. El hecho es que si nada se llega hacer al respecto, es probable que la relación no vaya a mejorar. Muchos harán la pregunta, "¿Porque no se va?" Pero la mayoría de las victimas en una relación saben que la solución no es nada fácil. Aquí hay algunas sugerencias que puedes tratar si la terapia no es la respuesta.

Aprende cuales son los recursos en su comunidad. Todas las comunidades tienen algún tipo de línea de crisis para hallar información sobre la violencia doméstica. Los consejeros de estas líneas de crisis están acostumbrados a tratar situaciones violentas y pueden proveer ideas y recursos. Ellos pueden referir a agencias o programas que le asistan. Muchas comunidades también tienen refugios que hospedan a mujeres y niños si deciden irse. Le ayudara el saber que usted no tiene que quedarse en una relación peligrosa o dolorosa. Usted tiene otras opciones. *Memoriza el número de teléfono de la línea de crisis.*

Aprende como la leyes sobre la violencia doméstica trabajan en su comunidad. Usted podrá recibir ayuda por medio de la policía o la corte, en casos de emergencia usar ordenes de protección, o ordenes de restricción, o otros instrumentos legales. Estas órdenes pueden ayudar a protegerla, pero recuerda que es solo un pedazo de papel. Una orden de restricción no servirá de nada si usted no esta dispuesta a reenforzarlo y llamar por ayuda cuando usted siente que no se puede proteger a si misma.

Ten un plan de seguridad. Esto es crucialmente importante. Si usted decide irse, usted necesita un plan. La mayoría de las mujeres son lastimadas más cuando deciden irse que en cualquier otra ocasión durante la relación. Sin un plan, la probabilidad de ser lastimada aumenta. Muchas mujeres que se van pronto regresan, y ellas pueden irse en varias ocasiones antes de finalmente permanecer distanciadas. Aunque este patrón de irse y regresar a la relación puede ser desanimante, no se de por vencida. No es fácil romper patrones de toda una vida. Vete cuantas veces crees necesitarlo, hasta que puedas permanecer distanciada del todo. Se lo mas claro posible sobre las cosas que la hacen ir y lo que la hacen regresar. Siendo honesta consigo misma es una parte importante en el proceso del crecimiento.

PLAN DE SEGURIDAD

Seguridad Durante un Incidente Explosivo

1. Si una discusión parece inevitable, trata de ir a un cuarto o una área donde este cerca de una salida. Trata de evadir los baños y las cocinas u otros lugares donde haya armas. En el baño, el agua, el secador, o las pinzas para encrespar, los pisos de mármol, y las porcelanas pueden ser utilizados como armas. También, los baños

usualmente tienen solo una salida y no permiten una salida o escape fácil e inmediata. Aun si tienes una puerta por atrás, la cocina sigue siendo peligrosa porque contiene acceso al fuego para quemar, el agua para hundir, y cuchillos, tenedores, licuadora, y otros objetos que pueden ser utilizados para lastimar.

2. Practica el salir segura de su casa. Identifica el camino que la sacara de la casa lo más rápido y segura.

3. Ten una maleta empacada y manténla guardada a la mano, como en la casa de una amiga. Con una maleta empacada, usted no tendrá que perder tiempo localizando artículos importantes, dándole al ofensor la oportunidad de convencerla de no irse-o de usted misma convencerse de no dejarlo.

4. Busce un vecino quien usted le pueda contar sobre la violencia y pidale que llame a la policía si el o ella escucha disturbios en su casa.

5. Desarrolla una señal de aviso para usar con sus hijos, familia, amistades, y vecinos para dejarles saber cuando usted necesita a la policía.

6. Planea a donde ir si usted se tuviera que salir de su casa, aun si piensa que usted no tendrá la necesidad de irse.

7. Utiliza sus propios instintos y juicio sabiamente. Si la situación es muy peligrosa, considera darle al ofensor lo que el quiere para calmarlo y espera un mejor momento para irse. Usted tiene el derecho de hacer lo que usted vea necesario para protegerse a si misma y a sus hijos hasta que usted este fuera de peligro.

Seguridad Cuando Se Prepara Irse

1. Abre una cuenta de ahorros en su propio nombre para obtener independencia económica. Piensa otras maneras de aumentar su independencia.

2. Deja dinero, un par de llaves de repuesto, copias de los documentos mas importantes, y una muda de ropa con alguien quien usted confía para que se pueda ir rápidamente.

3. Decida quien le pueda otorgar alojamiento o quien le pueda prestar algún dinero. No le diga a nadie que no sea su persona de confianza.

4. Mantenga el número telefónico de una casa de refugio a la mano. ¡Memorícelo!

5. Repasa con frecuencia su plan de seguridad. Cuando llegue el momento de irse, usted pueda que no este capacitada para pensar claramente y tendra que actuar automáticamente. Tracé y ponga en practica sus planes cuando usted este calmada y pueda pensar claramente.

Recuerda que el tiempo mas peligroso
es cuando usted decide irse.

Seguridad en Su Propia Casa

1. Si el ofensor deja el hogar, cambia las chapas de las puertas lo más pronto posible. Compra chapas adicionales y piezas que aseguren las ventanas.
2. Conversa el plan de seguridad con sus hijos para cuando no estés con ellos.
3. La escuela, guardería, y a las niñera de los niños deben ser informados, sobre quien tiene permiso de recogerlos y quien no deberá tener acceso a los niños.
4. Los vecinos y el propietario deben ser informados que su pareja ya no vive mas con usted y que deberán llamar a la policía si ellos lo ven cerca de la casa.

Seguridad con una Orden de Restricción

1. Averigua que ordenes de restricción están disponibles. Para hacerlo, usted debera llamar la oficina de abogados del distrito, la oficina de victimas, el servicio de abogados, o el departamento de policía.
2. Mantén la orden protectiva contigo en todo tiempo. En muchas comunidades, si usted tiene una orden de protección y llamas a la policía, ellos deben de llegar tan pronto sea posible. Sin una orden de protección, usted podrá tener dificultad de recibir ayuda cuando la necesite.
3. Llame la policía si su pareja de cualquier manera rompe la orden, sea por escrito, una llamada, o llendo a su trabajo o casa. No espere que la situación se haga mas violenta para llamar y buscar ayuda.
4. Sus amistades y familiares deben de estar informados que usted tiene una orden de protección. Insiste que ellos se pongan de

acuerdo para protegerla de su pareja. Esto requiere que ellos no esten dispuestos a mandar mensajes del ofensor pidiendo perdón ni dejar que el crea que su comportamiento es aceptable. Mas que todo, ellos no le pueden mencionar donde usted se encuentra. Dale una copia de la orden a una amiga, miembro de su familia, o terapista.

5. Se inteligente; recuerda, una orden de protección no previene que usted sea lastimada.

Seguridad en su Trabajo y en Público

1. Decide quien en el trabajo le piensas contar sobre la situación. Siempre debes de tener informado al vigilante de la oficina o del edificio.
2. Varía su rutina. Trata de coordinar que las llegadas y salidas y también las rutas hacia el trabajo sean diferentes.
3. Haz un plan de seguridad para cuando salgas del trabajo. Asegurase que alguien la acompañe a su auto o al auto-bus. Piensa lo que haría si algo le fuera a suceder en camino a su casa para así estar preparada a responder en caso de emergencia.

Su Seguridad y Salud Emocional

1. Si piensas regresar a una situación potencialmente abusiva, comparte un plan alternativo con alguien de confianza y quien respetas.
2. Si tienes que comunicar algo a su pareja, hazlo en la manera más segura posible, en un lugar público donde haya gente alrededor que la pueda proteger. Nunca este de acuerdo de meterse a un auto con su pareja, no vaya a un apartamento, casa, o oficina privada con el, y nunca vaya a una playa o parque aislada. Aunque usted crea que las cosas están bajo control y que usted las puede manejar, nunca ponga su seguridad a riesgo.
3. Practica pensamientos positivos sobre si misma y el ser asertiva con otros sobre sus necesidades. Usted necesita reconstruir su auto-estima.
4. Busca conserjería para usted y para sus hijos. Incluye grupos de apoyo para las victimas.

5. Decide con quien puedes hablar libremente y abiertamente para que tengas el apoyo que necesitas para permanecer segura.

Que Llevar Consigo Si Se Va

- Identificación
- Certificados de Nacimientos
- Libreta de banco
- La chequera
- Orden de Protección
- Medicinas
- Expedientes escolares
- Seguro Social
- Pasaporte
- Juguetes pequeños para niños
- Fotos y posesiones personales

- Licencia de conducir
- Dinero
- Papeles de la aseguranza
- Contrato de alquiler
- Libreta de teléfonos y direcciones
- Joyas
- Permiso de trabajo
- Identificación del Welfare
- Papeles de divorcio
- Llaves de la casa y del auto

Las preparaciones que usted haga antes de irse puede que sea la diferencia entre estar segura o exponerse al peligro. El prepararse bien puede ayudarla a sentirse fuerte y en control, asi usted podrá ser exitosa en su busqueda hacia la libertad.

Capítulo 6

Después Que Se Va

Finalmente haz logrado adquirir la valentía y los recursos para dejar la relación y ahora piensas en el porvenir. Al principio podrás tener muchos miedos y preocupaciones.

- ¿Se mantendrá retirado?
- ¿Me mantendré retirada?
- ¿Qué pasara cuando el quiera ver a los niños?

Con el tiempo, usted se sentirá aliviada y con energía. Aun sentirá mucha emoción, porque usted finalmente rompió el patrón del abuso. Eventualmente usted empezara a experimentar dolor por la perdida de su relación. En diversas temporadas, su dolor va involucrar diferentes emociones. Es apropiado sufrir la perdida de su relación, aunque reconozca que el terminar la relación fue lo mejor que pudo haber hecho. Usted sufrirá la perdida por el amor que tuvo, por el amor que pensó tener, o por el amor y la felicidad que usted espero crear. Usted sufrirá la perdida porque la relación no funciono. Tambien sufrirá la perdida de un sueño fallecido, de un cuento de hadas no realizada. Por eso es importante que se permita el tiempo y el espacio necesario para experimentar todas estas emociones. Este es el tiempo para sufrir su perdida y sanar. Usted podra sanar a medida que se permita sobrepasar el dolor.

Tomo catorce años para que Mariana finalmente decidiera dejar a su esposo. Por mucho tiempo, Mariana pensó que se sentiría bien recobrar la valentía de irse. Después de todo, ella había pasado muchos años sufriendo la perdida de una relación que ella quiso tener con su esposo. Aunque ella se preocupaba por su seguridad económica y de tener que lidiar con su ex-esposo sobre las vistas de los niños, ella no se había preocupado de su reacción emocional. Un poco después del rompimiento, Mariana se sorprendió y se molesto por haber extrañado a su esposo. Ella noto que se ponía a pensar sobre todas las cosas buenas y que poco a poco se iba desvaneciendo todas las memorias de los momentos infelices y violentos que vivió junto a el. Aproximadamente siete meses después del rompimiento, Mariana noto que ella extrañaba su esposo más que nunca. Mariana compartió sus sentimientos con un consejero quien la ayudo a identificar lo que en ese preciso momento marcaría sus quince años de aniversario de bodas. El consejero ayudo a que Mariana recordara las razones que la motivaron a que se fuera. El también retrazo los sentimientos de Mariana, ayudándole a ver que estos sentimientos eran memorias nostálgicas, las memorias que ella hubiera, obviamente, querido mantener. Pero el índico que estas memorias eran solo una pequeña porción del gran esquema y que las memorias y sentimientos que ella estaba experimentando no eran razón para regresar a una relación abusiva. Mariana pudo reconocer que ella necesitaba más tiempo para sufrir la perdida de su matrimonio. Estaba bien que ella estuviera triste, y era normal que ella se sintiera sola. Al reconocer y trabajar esos sentimientos, ella pronto pudo traspasarlos y aceptar que el rompimiento de la relación fue lo mejor que le pudo haber sucedido. A medida que su dolor se fue desvaneciendo, Mariana, por primera vez noto que desde su rompimiento, ella pudo pensar sobre su exesposo sin sentir odio ni ansias. Ella empezó a notar que habían otros hombres atractivos al su alrededor y que ella se sentía elogiada cuando un hombre en el trabajo empezaba a prestarle atención. Aunque ella no estaba preparada a tener otra pareja, Mariana reconoció que finalmente ella estaba dejando ir y sobrepasando su relación abusiva.

CONSTRUYENDO UNA RELACION CON SI MISMO

Con el tiempo usted pasara el susto, la tristeza, el enojo, y el alivio y llegara la preocupación por el futuro. Se preocupara de estar sola. Se preguntara si algunavez llegara a encontrar otra relación. Puede hasta que llegue a desconfiar su capacidad de elegir una pareja saludable. Se preocupara que nadie la va a querer. Todos estos pensamientos y sentimientos son normales y naturales; le suceden a todos que dejan una relación, abusiva o no abusiva.

El crecer en medio de sus preocupaciones y temores, requiere que usted se enfoque primeramente en si misma, que pueda poner a un lado la idea de tener otra relación. Permita que la relación precisa venga en el momento apropiado, cuando usted este lista. Por ahora es más importante aprender a estar sola. Saber enfrentar la soledad y el temor de una manera saludable, creando un sistema de apoyo de personas que verdaderamente la quieran, la respetan, y la apoyen a estar feliz con si misma.

Practica el querer ser buena consigo misma, empezando con la necesidad de reconstruir su auto-estima. Trata de tomar el tiempo y de ahorrar algo de dinero, si puedes, para dar un paseo especial o para comprar algo personal. Usted no tiene que gastar mucho dinero. Algunas cosas nuevas como una sobrecama para el cuarto, o algunas flores frescas, pueden hacer una gran diferencia en su vida. Aunque no tenga mucho dinero para gastar, se puede dar un trato especial al tomarse un largo baño en la tina, hacerse un vaso de chocolate caliente, o caminar en el parque. Haz una lista de todas las cosas que usted pueda pensar que la hará sentir bien y trata de hacer cuanto mas pueda por si misma todos los días. Con el tiempo, usted encontrara que su auto-estima y auto-valor regresará y empezará a reconocer que su relación con si misma es mas importante que cualquier otra relación que tenga.

CONSTUYENDO UNA RELACION CON OTRA PERSONA

Espero que usted se haya cuidado y, al a vez, empezado a trabajar sus asuntos o problemas en la terapia o en un grupo de apoyo. Suficiente tiempo ha pasado y usualmente requiere un mínimo de un año, para que puedas empezar a considerar la posibilidad de otra relación. ¿Como sabrás lo que es tener una buena relación? ¿Cómo puedes evitar el caer en otra relación abusiva? Los siguientes pasos le ayudaran a protegerse:

1. Haz una lista que explique el significado de lo que consiste una buena relación. Haz otra lista de señales que avisen cuando hay peligro de abuso. Coloque estas listas donde usted las pueda ver. Mírelas frecuentemente y meditelas. Cuando usted conozca a alguien, compare sus acciones con la lista así le ayudara a determinar objetivamente si esa persona es alguien la cual usted pueda considerar como pareja.

2. Cuando usted conozca a alguien por primera vez que le parezca interesante, ve despacio. Los primeros tres meses de la relación es un periodo de infatuación. Durante la infatuación usted no podrá ver la persona que es, usted solo vera lo que usted quiere ver en la persona. No haga ningún compromiso durante este periodo de tiempo. Si el la presiona muy rápidamente a involucrarse con el seriamente o comprometerse, deseé cuenta que esto puede ser una señal de aviso.

3. Mire sus acciones. Acuérdese que las palabras, promesas, o explicaciones son fáciles, y en realidad no dicen quien es su pareja. Ponle menos valor a sus palabras y mas valor a lo que hace y como se comporta. Nota si lo que dice sobre el pasado llega a ser cierto. Nota si el cumple sus promesas. Nota sus acciones, no sus palabras.

4. Pida el conocer otras personas que han estado en su vida-su familia, amigos, compañeros de trabajo, y aun su jefe. Mira la manera que el interactúa con estas personas. Observa cuales son sus reacciones hacia el. ¿Observa si ellos demuestran amor, afecto, y aceptación hacia el? ¿Acaso dicen cosas buenas de el? ¿Acaso parece que ellos tratan de darle alguna advertencia a que se cuide? Si el evade en sacarla a pasar tiempo con sus amistades o miembros de su familia, reconozca que el evadir es motivo de precaución; el claramente esconde algo importante que no tendría que esconder si el fuese una persona honesta y abierta, y en búsqueda de una relación significante y real.

5. Llevalo a que conozca a su familia, amistades, y compañeros de trabajo. Pregúntales honestamente lo que piensan sobre el. *Toma las opiniones de la familia y de las amistades seriamente.* Recuerda que ellos no tratan de detener su felicidad; ellos solo tratan de protegerla de su propio patrón enfermizo. Si ellos expresan preocupación o no llegan a aprobar su relación, esto no significa que debes dejar la relación, pero si es una señal que debes considerar con mucha precaución esa relación antes de involucrarse. Usted no tiene que dejar que su familia o que sus amistades elijan su relación, pero ellos la han observado en otras relaciones y conocen los tipos de problemas que uno tiende a tener al elegir una relación saludable.

Recuerda que su familia y amistades no están bajo el velo de la ilusión e infatuación que pueda estar encubriendo sus ojos. Ellos podrán ver la potencialidad de los problemas de una manera más realista y más claro de lo que puedas ver en el presente. Aunque solo sean pocas las personas en su vida que expresen preocupación y duda sobre su interés romántico, es importante tomar estas preocupaciones y dudas seriamente. Usted pueda que quiera continuar la relación. Si esto es lo que decide hacer, toma las preocupaciones de sus amistades y su familia seriamente y con precaución. Asegurese de prestarle atención a los comportamientos que han causado preocupación en aquellos que amas.

Si su interés amoroso evade el conocer a sus amistades y familiares o si el se incomoda de tener que compartir su compañía con ellos, reconoce que estos son comportamientos peligrosos.

6. Espera aunque sea un año antes de comprometerse a vivir o casarse con su nueva pareja. Un año provee el tiempo que se necesita para observarlo en diversas situaciones. Usted necesita tiempo para que la infatuación desvanezca y pueda empezar a ver la verdadera persona que le interesa. Mira lo que el hace cuando algo triste o estresante le sucede, y como el reacciona cuando usted esta triste o estresada. Mira lo que sucede cuando el se enoja con alguien y lo que sucede cuando el se enoja contigo. Trata de confrontar honestamente su reacción ante situaciones y no acepte o haga excusas por el. Mide su comportamiento con la lista. Si el no cubre los requisitos de la lista, debes de estar dispuesta a dejar la relación ahora, antes que se profundice.

7. Préstale atención a sus sentimientos y reacciones intuitivos. Estos sentimientos son clave en mantener su seguridad. Si se siente "mal," "con miedo," "culpable," "sin valor," "equivocada," o "enojada" en su relación, eso significa que usted no se esta cuidando a si misma. Usted se preocupa más por las necesidades y sentimientos de el que por los suyos. Esto es el primer pasó hacia una relación peligrosa. Si usted experimenta sentimientos negativos, su relación necesitara una evaluación. Aunque sea cierto que toda relación tiene problemas, y que la mayoría de las parejas tienen desacuerdos, en una relación saludable los problemas, asuntos, o desacuerdos pueden ser resueltos sin que se sienta mal de si misma, y sin ser físicamente lastimada.

8. Contrario a lo que puedas pensar ahora, no es cierto que todas las parejas pelean o que toda relación requiere un trabajo constante. Lo que es cierto es que toda pareja tiene sus diferencias y

desacuerdos y que toda relación en algún momento necesitara atención.

Para tomar una buena decisión sobre una nueva relación, usted debe asegurarse de ver las siguientes señales que compone una relación saludable.

1. El la respeta como una persona separada e independiente. El la trata con igualdad, sin hacerla menos que el o superior a el. El respeta su privacidad y los limites que trazas para su propia comodidad y seguridad.
2. El le interesa escuchar sobre sus sentimientos, opiniones, e intereses. El quiere formar parte de su vida y hace el esfuerzo de llegar a conocer sus amistades y familiares.
3. El pregunta su opinión al hacer decisiones que le puedan afectar. El considera sus sentimientos y opiniones como si fueran legítimos y los valora cuando no estas de acuerdo.
4. El la apoya emocionalmente cuando pasa por un problema o se encuentra con mucha tensión. Usted puede contar con que el sea cariñoso y colaborador cuando confrontes algún problema. El nunca utiliza sus momentos de debilidad o secretos compartidos para manipular, castigar, o tomar ventaja.
5. El solo quiere compartir una igualdad en su relación sexual. El no esta interesado en manipularla o forzarla a tener sexo cuando usted se sienta incomoda.
6. El no le tiene miedo a las diferencias que existen entre ustedes y esta dispuesto a negociar y comprometerse para llegar a un acuerdo en que los dos estén cómodos.
7. El apoya su éxito personal, profesional y económico. El esta orgulloso de y no se siente amenazado por sus logros.
8. El maneja sus propios sentimientos negativos y reacciones en una manera honesta y madura. Cuando el se enoja o se molesta, el se puede expresar sin culpar, criticar o recurrir a las amenazas o a la violencia física.
9. El es responsable de su estado económico.
10. El es capaz de mantener su propia identidad y al vez se dispone a compartir su vida con su pareja.

Usted pudo haber sufrido tanto dolor en su relación, que su nuevo temor seria el no poder reconocer una buena relación o el no permitir que alguien se acerque a usted aunque sea una persona buena y amorosa. Por lo tanto, trata de respetar sus propias preocupaciones y temores, utilizelas para que le ayuden a recordar cuan precavida debes de ser sobre una unión prematura. Cuando usted empiece a interesarse por otra persona ve despacio. Si usted ha elegido una persona madura, responsable, y amorosa el entenderá porque estas a la defensiva, estará dispuesto a trabajar contigo, y daría el tiempo que necesites para construir su confianza en el. Si el es impaciente, la crítica, o hace burla de sus temores, el no es la persona para usted. Después de algunos meses de estar en una relación segura, usted notara que ha empezado a bajar su guardia, confiando mas en el y en si misma. Si después de algunos meses usted aun se siente con miedo y esta en guardia, busca la guía y la ayuda de un consejero profesional. El consejero le ayudara a ver la diferencia entre sus propios temores y las cosas que parecen ser causa de una gran preocupación. Si se siente segura en su relación pero a la vez tiene mucho temor de llegar a algo mas intimo, la terapia le ayudara a sobrepasar estos temores al explorar los riesgos que habitan en el deseo de amar otra vez.

SUS HIJOS

Mientras este aprendiendo a cuidarse a si misma, usted también tendrá niños de quien preocuparse. Sus hijos podrán tener los mismos sentimientos y reacciones al dejar el ambiente abusivo en la que vivían. Lo más importante para sus hijos al hacer el ajuste de irse es como usted vaya a manejar la situación. Usted puede ayudar a que el cambio sea mas comodo para sus hijos, comportandose de una manera calmada, asegurandoles que usted esta en control y que usted se encargara de todo.

Sus hijos pasaran por un proceso de muchas perdidas. Ellos podrán estar muy tristes, enojados, temerosos, felices, aliviados, o preocupados por el futuro como lo esta usted. Mas sín embargo, ellos pueda que no tengan los mismos sentimientos que los suyos.

Sus hijos tendrán sus propias experiencias con su pareja. Ellos podrán no haber sido personalmente abusados. El ofensor puede haber manipulado sus pensamientos, creencias, y sentimientos, así como el manipulo los suyos. Sus hijos pueden estar confusos y a la vez atemorizados en su decisión de irse.

Recuerda que sus hijos pueden querer al ofensor y pueda que sea duro para ellos entender porque no se pueden quedar con el. Ellos podrán quererlo aunque hayan sido abusados. Usted tendrá que respetar los sentimientos que tengan sus hijos y a la vez trazar límites y barreras que sean saludables para ellos. Diles que esta bien el amar a su padre (como sea la relación) pero que no esta bien que los maltrate. Se firme cuando le digas que no es aceptable que ellos lastimen o abusen a alguien, no importa cuan enojados estén o cual sea la razón. Estos mensajes son muy importantes para sus hijos porque ellos pudieron aprender de lo observado en la relación. Que la manipulación, control y el abuso son maneras de lograr lo que quieren. El decirle a sus niños que, usted y ellos, merecen ser tratados con amor y que usted no se quedara con alguien que sea abusivo es muy importante.

Sus hijos se podrán enojar por haberse ido y podrán culparla por todos los problemas que han ocurrido en la familia. Trata de no tomar su enojo personal. Muchas veces es más fácil y más seguro que los niños se enojen con la victima, la persona más débil de la familia, que al ofensor quien ellos suelen temer. Si ellos expresan enojo y culpabilidad hacia usted, eso significa que ellos han logrado sentirse lo suficíentemente seguros para expresar lo que sienten sin temor a la violencia.

Trata de no ponerse a la defensiva si sus hijos expresan culpabilidad o enojo hacia usted, pero si es necesario trazar limites si sus hijos tratan de abusarla verbalmente o físicamente. Es bueno decirle a los niños que usted respeta sus sentimientos y que esta bien si ellos quieren hablar sobre ellos. Sin embargo, es importante que usted cree haber tomado la mejor decisión para todos, y que esperas que ellos puedan respetar la decisión aunque ellos no estén de acuerdo.

Los hijos muchas veces tienen dificultad al hablar sobre sus sentimientos o el mostrar sus emociones. Ellos podrán actuar como si nada hubiese ocurrido y podrán hacer lo suyo como niños, jugando cuando puedan y saliendo con sus amigos cuando se les permite. No cometa el error de pensar que el irse no les va a molestar. Al contrario, observa cuidadosamente las señales de angustia en sus hijos y ayúdelos a expresar sus sentimientos sobre la situación.

Aquí hay algunas cosas que usted puede hacer para ayudar a que sus hijos expresen sus sentimientos:

1. Si sus hijos expresan angustia sea verbalmente o por medio de su comportamiento, usted podría decirles, "Yo estoy notando que usted esta (enojado/triste/con medio). Yo me pregunto si se sienten de esa manera porque nosotros hemos dejado (a papa). Yo siento algunos de los mismos sentimientos. Alo mejor nosotros podemos hablar sobre eso."

2. Si sus hijos no quieren hablar, usted podría decirles, "Yo noto que ustedes se sienten (tristes/con miedo/enojados). . . . Yo quiero que sepas que está bien que tengan sentimientos y yo estaré aquí si quieren hablar sobre ellos."

3. Si sus hijos no quieren hablar sobre sus sentimientos o sobre la situación, anímalos a que lo escriban o lo dibujen. Provéeles algunos juguetes que les permitan expresar sus sentimientos por medio del juego, tales como el jugar a la casa, o a el policía si es que la policía se involucro en detener la violencia. Si sus hijos están enojados, les puede ayudar a tener acceso a un bate de béisbol de corcho o un bulto de harina. Al darle a sus hijos disversas maneras de expresar sus sentimientos le indicara que usted realmente los entiende y respeta.

4. Si sus niños aparentan querer hablar pero no quieren hablar contigo, pregúntales con quien estarían dispuestos hablar, y así les ayudas hacer un arreglo para que puedan tener tiempo con esa persona en privado. Déjales saber a sus hijos que está bien si ellos no quieren hablar contigo—usted quiere respetar su privacidad y sus sentimientos—pero es importante que ellos le hablen a alguien para que sus sentimientos no se acumulen ni se lastimen por dentro.

5. Si sus hijos no están hablando sobre su enojo o tristeza pero si se están aislando; regresando a comportamiento infantil o apegándose a usted; se orinan o defecan después de haber sido entrenados a ir al baño, pegándoles a otros niños, o sus hábitos al comer, dormir, jugar, o estudiar han sido interrumpidos, consigue ayuda profesional para ellos. Un consejero puede ayudar a que su hijo encuentre maneras saludables para expresar sus sentimientos y reacciones emocionales. Por el momento, no permita que en este tiempo sus hijos se mal acostumbren o estén fuera de control. Continua a trazar limites firmes y constantes para prevenir que ellos sean destructivos con si mismos, con usted, y hacia otros, incluyendo a los animales o posesiones de mucha importancia.

Recuerda que la cosa más importante y necesaria para sus hijos en este momento es que vean que usted puede manejar las cosas, y saber que los ama y se preocupa como les pueda afectar los cambios. Al actuar calmadamente, firmemente, y al tomar cualquier oportunidad para asegurarles que su amor por ellos nunca desvanecerá, usted podrá ayudarles en cada situación.

Sus hijos han estado creciendo en una familia enfermiza. Han visto y aprendido patrones de pensamientos y comportamientos que no son saludables. Tal como usted necesita crecer libre, también ellos. Usted es la llave de su libertad para que lleguen a ser adultos saludables y cariñosos. Ustedes pueden llegar a crecer juntos hacia la libertad.

NOTAS

NOTAS

NOTAS

NOTAS

Índice

CRECIENDO LIBRE

Manual para Sobrevivientes de la Violencia Doméstica

_____in softbound at $11.21 (regularly $14.95) (ISBN: 0-7890-1899-3)

Or order online and use Code HEC25 in the shopping cart.

COST OF BOOKS_____	☐ **BILL ME LATER:** ($5 service charge will be added)
	(Bill-me option is good on US/Canada/Mexico orders only; not good to jobbers, wholesalers, or subscription agencies.)
OUTSIDE US/CANADA/ MEXICO: ADD 20%_____	
POSTAGE & HANDLING_____	☐ Check here if billing address is different from shipping address and attach purchase order and billing address information.
(US: $5.00 for first book & $2.00 for each additional book) Outside US: $6.00 for first book) & $2.00 for each additional book)	
	Signature_____
SUBTOTAL_____	☐ **PAYMENT ENCLOSED: $**_____
IN CANADA: ADD 7% GST_____	☐ **PLEASE CHARGE TO MY CREDIT CARD.**
STATE TAX_____	☐ Visa ☐ MasterCard ☐ AmEx ☐ Discover
(NY, OH & MN residents, please add appropriate local sales tax)	☐ Diner's Club ☐ Eurocard ☐ JCB
	Account # _____
FINAL TOTAL_____	Exp. Date_____
(If paying in Canadian funds, convert using the current exchange rate, UNESCO coupons welcome)	Signature_____

Prices in US dollars and subject to change without notice.

NAME_____

INSTITUTION_____

ADDRESS_____

CITY_____

STATE/ZIP_____

COUNTRY_____ COUNTY (NY residents only)_____

TEL_____ FAX_____

E-MAIL_____

May we use your e-mail address for confirmations and other types of information? ☐ Yes ☐ No
We appreciate receiving your e-mail address and fax number. Haworth would like to e-mail or fax special discount offers to you, as a preferred customer. **We will never share, rent, or exchange your e-mail address or fax number.** We regard such actions as an invasion of your privacy.

Order From Your Local Bookstore or Directly From
The Haworth Press, Inc.
10 Alice Street, Binghamton, New York 13904-1580 • USA
TELEPHONE: 1-800-HAWORTH (1-800-429-6784) / Outside US/Canada: (607) 722-5857
FAX: 1-800-895-0582 / Outside US/Canada: (607) 771-0012
E-mailto: orders@haworthpress.com
PLEASE PHOTOCOPY THIS FORM FOR YOUR PERSONAL USE.
http://www.HaworthPress.com

conduct a ten-minute debriefing when they returned the completed map. We gave the student full-color, 11- by 17-inch maps of campus and asked them to record where they went during a weekday as they were actually experiencing it (see Fig. 7.1). These diaries recorded the times and sequence of each event. After the students completed their maps, they were interviewed by the River Campus Libraries' lead anthropologist. The interviews were tape-recorded and later transcribed.

In a second round of diaries, we wanted to target students who lived off campus. In fall 2006, we posted flyers in the science and engineering library inviting students who lived off campus to keep a mapping diary. As with the first round of mapping diaries, we interviewed the five students about their maps and transcribed the interviews.

Across the two rounds of diaries, our recruitment methods yielded a varied group of students, both male and female, from freshmen to upperclassmen, and in a wide range of majors.

Sample Diary

It is hard to describe a "typical" student day, but the following timeline—of a busy senior majoring in a scientific field—is representative. Like the majority of University of Rochester students, he lives on campus. The information in this timeline comes from the interview conducted with the student. We have removed identifying information (Kaplan 2006).

8:30 A.M.: Leaves his dorm and goes to the main campus computer center, located on the ground

floor of the main humanities and social sciences library, to finish up some homework for the day.

11:00 A.M.: Goes from the computer center to a classroom building to meet with a professor during office hours to discuss classwork.

12:30 P.M.: Goes to a political science class in a second classroom building.

1:40 P.M.: Walks back to first classroom building to talk with the same professor. The student works in the professor's lab, so this time they talk about his job, not his class.

2:00 P.M.: Goes back to the computer center again to meet a group of friends and do homework. They like the mezzanine level of the computing center, which has large eight-seater tables and chairs—"It's good place to do group study."

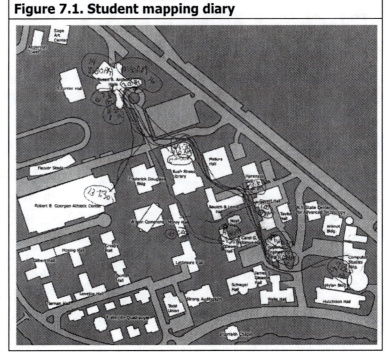

Figure 7.1. Student mapping diary

3:00 P.M.: Walks back to his dorm room for a quick meal. He is not on a meal plan but has a fridge in his room. He eats quick prepackaged food that he can "go in and grab" for lunch.

3:25 P.M.: Walks from dorm to classroom building for class.

4:40 P.M.: Goes from one classroom to another in the same building for a third class.

6:00 P.M.: Walks to another classroom building for third class in a row, the fourth class of the day.

7:00 P.M.: Walks back to a previous classroom building to work on an assignment.

7:30 P.M.: Back to his dorm room, not to eat dinner, but to change clothes for the gym.

7:45 P.M.: Walks to the campus athletic center and works out at the gym for 45 minutes.

8:30 P.M.: Back to dorm to shower.

9:00 P.M.: Goes to science and engineering library to meet a couple of other people and study.

12:30 A.M.: Goes back to his dorm and finally eats dinner.

Using a scaled map of the campus, we measured the distances from building to building, "as the crow flies," to calculate how far the student walked. In this actual day, this student covered approximately 2.5 miles just walking back and forth across our relatively small campus (Kaplan 2006).

What Did We Learn?

Although each student's diary was unique, by examining all fourteen we began to see some commonalities:

1. Students do more than just attend classes. Even when students report going to one or more classes, they participate in a surprising number of other activities. The number and variety of different activities seem notable especially given that this reflects the movements of only fourteen students. In addition to going to class, our fourteen students

- Went to science and engineering labs
- Went to language conversation lab
- Went to recitation
- Had jobs
- Studied, read, and did homework
- Met professors during office hours
- Went to the gym to work out
- Practiced fencing
- Practiced karate
- Rode their bikes
- Walked or biked or took the bus to class
- Ran
- Ate at campus dining facilities, in their dorm, at home, on the bus, in class, at work, in the library, in the lab, off campus
- Checked their mail at the campus post office
- Went to the registrar's office
- Met friends to study with at the library and the computer center
- Studied by themselves at the library
- Checked e-mail at the computer center
- Met with tutors at the writing center
- Went to jazz rehearsal
- Practiced clarinet
- Participated in clubs
- Attended sorority and fraternity events

- Watched television in their dorm room
- Attended lectures at nearby colleges
- Went off campus to eat and shop
- Attended church services

Some of these activities—such as going to a lab or to work—do not surprise us. Other activities do. For example, many students who completed maps indicated that they exercise. Some got up early to go to the gym or run. One did karate for several hours in the evening. In addition, the students walked a considerable distance crisscrossing campus. The University of Rochester is a heavily residential campus, and though a few students did go off campus to shop, eat, or attend lectures at a nearby college, the majority stayed on campus all day and walked sometimes several miles on the day they mapped out.

2. Students are highly scheduled and on the go all the time. Our students are on the run all day and many of them late into the night. The majority of students we interviewed left their dorm rooms early in the morning and did not return until after dinner. Many checked their e-mail during breaks between classes. Some of the freshmen went back to their dorm briefly, most of them just to drop off books and pick up what they needed for the next part of the day. They had little down time according to their diaries and interviews. For example, one student said, "Generally on a typical day I leave [dorm room] in the morning and I won't go back unless I forget something until the evening."

3. Students' schedules are "offset" from librarians' schedules. Most of us are at our best between 8 A.M. and 8 P.M. and at full concentration between 11 A.M. and 1 P.M. Students who competed maps were up at 8 A.M. but on the go until 1 or 2 A.M. In fact, only two of the students we interviewed got up later than 8:30. Two students were exercising (running or in

the gym) by 7 A.M. But, more important, not only are they awake much later than most librarians (at least this author) are, they did productive work long after we had left the library. Our analysis of the maps leads up to conclude that students' peak concentration time is much later than ours, typically between 10 P.M. and 1 A.M. They do some work such as finishing up homework for class during the day, mostly at odd hours between classes; but their concentrated work blocks are after 10 P.M. As one student commented, "I think it's pretty typical. You always end up doing most of your work in the library late at night. Not necessarily that late, but definitely in the evening hours is when most people do the serious studying. You might do a little bit before classes, but you don't get serious until after dinner usually."

4. Students eat on the go. Most students who completed the mapping diaries did not eat regular meals. They ate at odd times, often just snacking wherever they were. Few of them ate more than one "real" meal during their typical day on the run. They brought food with them to eat in the library, in lab, in class, on the bus, and at work. Fond memories of sitting down with everyone in our dorm in the dining hall and eating dinner together have long faded. What we see now is that students eat quick meals of such prepackaged food as oatmeal in their dorm rooms. When they do eat a real meal, most of them do so on campus. In our mapping group, few students left campus to eat or had food delivered.

5. Students carry their belonging with them, but not their laptops. Students reported carrying stuff with them during the day—everything from books and notebooks to food, energy drinks, and even a bike frame for use in a presentation. One student we interviewed carried his clarinet because he used the music practice rooms in a building on campus and did not want to take the time to go back to his apartment off campus. Some of the freshmen popped back to their dorm rooms to pick up textbooks for their next class or change clothes before they went to the gym. What they did not carry with them were their laptops. None of the students we interviewed brought their laptops with them from the dorms. The students explained that they were too heavy to lug all over campus and, because of their value, it was very inconvenient to keep them secure, as was confirmed by several of the student interviews:

> **Student:** I don't need my laptop, just 'cause I base everything that I—anything that I'm going to need on campus, I'll just send to my e-mail account so I can just access it right away. But other than that, it is easier to just keep my backpack full of my books and binders, and it's not too heavy.

> **Interviewer:** Do you carry your laptop around ever?

> **Student:** No, well not never, but this entire year I carried it around three or four times because it weighs a ton. I should have bought a better one.

6. Students use computer technology throughout the day and in multiple locations. Although the students do not carry their laptops with them, they did use such technology all throughout the day. They depended on the computers in the computer lab and in the library to check e-mail and to use them to "do homework."

7. Students study in the library, at home/in their dorms, and in the computer lab. The majority of students reported doing at least some studying during the day at the library. "Library is really the center of everything you do. It's where you go between classes, it's like … it serves as the function of your room. It's where you go between classes when you are not eating. You are only in your room really in the morning and when you go to bed." The prevalence of the library may have been in part because some of our recruitment strategies pulled from library users. Other study locations were mentioned, including dorm rooms, the campus computing center, in classroom buildings, at their job, in the lab, and at the student union.

8. There is no "average" day for a student. Of course, we have to be careful to generalize too much from these diaries because there is no "average" day. These days were described variously as "my easy day," "the day I'm totally slammed," and "a really, busy day." The students indicated that their class, work, and social schedules vary from day to day. None of our diaries reflected student activities on the weekends, which also would be interesting to learn about.

Implications for Academic Libraries

It has been interesting for us just to know more about what students do during the day, but these observations also have important implications for our library facilities and services.

Study Space

We learned that most students do study in the library, and that many of them view the library as the "center" of their day. This means that our library facilities need to accommodate all the different activities students are trying to do during they day. They want a place to study, to check their e-mail, to meet their friends, to read, to write their papers, to kill time between classes, and to eat. Their ideal library would allow them to do all of these things easily under one roof.

We learned from the interviews that students prefer a variety of settings to study in, depending on what kind of activity they are doing. Sometimes they are in the library for a long period of time, sometimes only briefly. Some students like to work at big tables with friends; others spread their work out in a quiet area or confine themselves in the solitude of a small study carrel. There are students who work quietly with friends and others who want to talk and laugh with their friends. No one size fits all. Consequently, libraries need to be mindful of this and try to provide students with a variety of environments to support their academic work preferences, which include spaces to accommodate social times and breaks.

Because we saw that students wanted a variety of different kinds of study space, we created a webpage that details the different kinds of spaces to be found in the main library.[1] The page lists quiet places, collaborative places, comfy seats, public workstations, electrical outlets for laptops, and future spaces. Moreover, our observation that no one size fits all led us to seek more feedback from students about their space needs. To help with the design of a major renovation in the main humanities and social sciences library, we ran two design workshops in which we asked students to draw their ideal library space (see Chapter 4).

Technology

Although students carried all kinds of things with them, including a bike frame, none of the students we interviewed carried a laptop. This does not mean that they are without computer access during the day. Students used computers in the library and campus computing labs. They checked their e-mail, did homework, looked up articles, used a program to turn in their math homework, and just "browsed." Over the past few years, our library has discussed getting rid of our public computers, because "every student has a laptop." Yes, most of

them do have laptops, but we saw clearly through the diaries that they still expect us to provide them with desktop computing support.

We confirmed that students do a lot of their academic work from their dorm rooms. This serves to reinforce our commitment to making as many library resources as possible available electronically and remotely.

It also was clear that students do not understand that the computer lab, which is housed in the physical library building, is not part of the library. It is obvious to library and computing staff that the two entities are different, but not to students. We now understand a little better why students are confused, surprised, and sometimes disappointed when the library computers do not have the same software and functionality as the workstations in the computer center. Because of this project, providing access to an identical desktop and suite of services became a top priority for the library and will be fully implemented by the fall 2007 semester.

Food and Drink

We learned that undergraduates often eat on the run. The libraries at the University of Rochester have allowed food and drink in the building for many years. After reviewing these interview transcripts, we wonder whether our open food and drink policy might be a contributing factor to the heavy use made of the library, especially by undergraduates. One could easily imagine that, if food and drink were not allowed in the library, it would be a much less attractive and convenient place for undergraduates to come to work, study, or hang out.

Hours of Service

We learned quite a bit from these interviews that can help us better understand how students use the reference desk. We know that students come to the reference desk in the evening, looking for articles for a paper that is due tomorrow. Are they all procrastinators? Probably some are, but that is only part of the answer. Instead, it is clear that students are very scheduled and on the go all day. They may not have any free time until 9 P.M. or later to come and ask a reference librarian for help, but unfortunately 9 P.M. is typically when our reference desks close. Many, if not all of us, have seen a decrease in the number of face-to-face reference questions. Could it be that undergraduates do not ask us questions at the reference desk because we are not staffing the desk when (and where) they are writing their papers, that is, after nine at night? How can they come ask a question at the reference desk which typically closes at nine? How can they attend a library workshop typically offered during the afternoon when they are already so busy during the day? Many library services, with the exception of circulation, which is open from early in the morning (8 A.M.) until early the next morning (3 A.M.), are clearly out of step with students' schedules and require some careful reconsideration.

We have made some changes in response to what we learned from the mapping diaries. For example, we were struck by the disconnect between the hours of reference service and the time of day when students do their work. Our response was to establish Night Owl Librarian service, which extended our reference desk hours several nights a week during the busiest weeks of the semester (see Chapter 3). We felt it was important to try to provide reference service at the time of day when students could more easily use it.

Support for Students Who Live off Campus

The students who live off campus have several different strategies for storing their belongings. One student e-mails everything to himself so he does not need to carry his laptop with him. Two of the students had on campus jobs and used their offices as their home away from home. One of these students stashes books, food, silverware, and even interview clothes at her workplace; the other goes back to his workplace several times a day to pick up things: "I sort of live there [at work], it is sort of my home. I leave all my books and everything I don't need and I go back and pick it up anytime I want."

Again, providing computer access, allowing food and drink, and probably providing a place to store books and coats would better support the students who live off campus. Long before we conducted this study, the science and engineering library purchased textbooks for reserve. Reflecting on what we have learned, it has probably been very helpful for students to find their textbooks in the library rather than having to lug them with them from home or from their dorm rooms.

Conclusion

When we started this project, we knew very little about what undergraduates did during the day other than go to class and come to the library. We did not have a sense for what their schedules or days were like. After asking fourteen students to keep track of their daily activity on a campus map and following up with an in-person interview, we have a much better sense of their lives. They are busy and heavily scheduled. They get up early but do not start their academic work until late at night.

These mapping diaries are just one piece of the larger Undergraduate Research Project undertaken by the River Campus Libraries. Our overarching goal was to understand how students "do their work," and this included when and where they study. These mapping diaries proved to be a rich source of insight about student lives and have led directly to some initial changes to be more responsive to our students' needs.

Note

1. http://www.lib.rochester.edu/index.cfm?PAGE=3469.

eight. What an Experience: Library Staff Participation in Ethnographic Research

Helen Anderson and Ann Marshall

Why would an academic library attempt to study its students? A typical answer would include discovering new insights about our students and then using these to inform library planning. Indeed, our Undergraduate Research Project led to made many informative discoveries, some of which are discussed in other chapters of this book. In addition to these, our project has had a more immediate impact on the staff who participated. In this chapter we focus on how the methodologies used in the project helped to create an environment conducive to generating new perspectives, which in turn has affected staff members' day-to-day work.

In gathering data for this chapter, we informally interviewed twelve project participants, asking each a series of questions about their involvement in the project. In the first part of this chapter, we discuss the kinds of tasks that staff engaged in during the undergraduate project as well as some of the underlying ethnographic and work-practice methodologies used. In the second part of the chapter we explain how participation in the study resulted in important changes in staff interactions with students and view their own academic role within the library. Specifically, we focus on our interactions with students at the reference desk and in the classroom. All of this is presented in the hope that readers will be encouraged to experiment with similar methods in their own professional settings.

Project Participation: Who, When, and How

Given significant demands on library staff time, some readers may ask if their own schedules could accommodate a two-year study of this scope. Our project was, however, structured to be attentive to staff schedules. We aimed to be as open as possible to staff involvement at all levels and from all departments while offering a wide variety of ways that staff could meaningfully participate. This included the option of occasionally attending a one-hour meeting or helping out with the preparation and execution of some of the project's exercises. Staff more deeply involved in the project negotiated time for participation with their own supervisors.

By the end of the study, the project was able to involve approximately 30 percent of the staff at the University of Rochester's River Campus Libraries. This number includes staff from technical services, reference departments in the humanities, social sciences, and science libraries, circulation, collection development, administration, interlibrary loan, acquisitions, and digital initiatives. Participants' job titles included subject librarian, library assistant, Web designer, anthropologist, department head, science and engineering library director, and associate dean.

A core group of three librarians and an anthropologist developed a project plan and organized and planned meetings. A larger proj-

Helen Anderson is Head, Collection Development at the River Campus Libraries, University of Rochester; e-mail: handerson@library.rochester.edu. Ann Marshall is Political Science Subject Librarian at the River Campus Libraries, University of Rochester; e-mail: amarshall@library.rochester.edu

ect team of ten staff members met for an hour and a half each month to advise the core group, participate in interviews, and, in later stages of the project, view and discuss data. In addition, the three subteams (reference outreach, digital initiatives, and facilities) ensured that important research questions were addressed in each of these three areas, helped plan research projects, then viewed data and shared it with others involved in the research. The subteams often met weekly or biweekly, and it was through their activities that many other library staff were able to participate on a more casual basis as their schedules allowed.

At the start of the project, an open invitation was made at a general staff meeting, and volunteers signed up for one or another group depending on their interests. Throughout the project, calls were issued for additional volunteers to perform tasks such as running the video camera during an interview, viewing data with a group of staff, proofreading interview transcripts, and coding data. Participants received training from the project's lead anthropologist.

Throughout the project, we engaged in several different techniques in order to immerse ourselves in the data and capture our thoughts and ideas. Three of these techniques were especially important in giving us access to the perspectives of students: observation and listening techniques, coviewing, and brainstorming.

Observing and Listening

In the initial stages of the project, staff participants completed an exercise that involved positioning themselves discreetly in pairs in a public place of their choice and observing the activity taking place there for a set period of time. Many people chose stores or malls, and one group sat on the bus that runs between two university campuses. We all took notes and then met with our partners to discuss our observations. Later we met

as a larger group to discuss our experiences with the exercise. The goal here was to give the staff members an experience of basic anthropological methods, particularly observation and note taking. We learned to simply observe and listen, without feeling the need to rush in to fix a situation or answer a question. We experienced the process of observing and taking notes as separate from that of forming an opinion about a situation or activity. Holding the video camera during an interview also provided opportunities to practice intentional observation and listening.

Coviewing and Discussing

Coviewing is a technique used to bring people together in a setting where data from the study can be collectively viewed and discussed (see Suchman and Triff 1991; Brun-Cottan and Wall 1995). In our case, staff involved in the project were brought together to watch videotaped interviews of students jointly and then engage in discussions about content from the interviews. Since two people at most were present during the actual interview, coviewing allowed us to involve a greater number of staff in the project. In addition, we could become immersed in the data with minimal demands on our time.

The viewings sponsored by the reference outreach subteam are a useful illustration of how these sessions were organized. Reference outreach coviewing meetings were advertised by e-mail to all reference staff and were held over the lunch hour to provide a time slot that most staff could attend. There was no obligation to attend, and staff could choose to come to one, many, or none of these meetings. The subteam sponsored coviewing meetings twice a month for roughly a five-month period. Attendance varied from four to nine library staff, with some staff attending only once and others attending the majority of the sessions.

These sessions provided staff members with access to the data collected from and about

Figure 8.1. Brainstorming session in progress

our undergraduate population.[1] The majority of materials collected for this project, with the exception of the design workshops (see Chapter 5), had a corresponding interview, including both audio and video. The goal of coviewing was not, however, simply to listen and watch the interview. The technique of coviewing also involves mechanisms to encourage staff to share their reactions to the interview. This was accomplished, first, by giving some initial guidance about the types of reactions best suited for coviewing. The premise underlying these coviewing sessions was that learning about student experiences from the student point of view is valuable. Therefore, the goal was not to critique the student but to try, as best as possible, to get into the student's head and then to remark on issues that surprised us or that we did not previously know. In addition, staff were encouraged to remark on questions raised by the interview and insights the interview gave us about our own work.

Staff were instructed that, if they wanted to make a remark, they should raise their hand or ask that the video be stopped. We found that we quickly became comfortable with this practice, and in a typical one-hour session we would watch about thirty minutes of video, interspersed with four or five breaks for a total of

twenty minutes of conversation. The remaining ten minutes were used for setup, introductory instructions, and logistics. We aimed to create a fun, comfortable, and interesting environment for the coviewing sessions. One librarian remarked that what she enjoyed most about coviewing was experiencing her own reactions while at the same time hearing others' perspectives.

Brainstorming

One final technique that had a large impact on staff was brainstorming. Brainstorming sessions helped staff to generate an extensive list of ideas about student needs and what we as staff wished we could accomplish. Brainstorming sessions led to specific pilot projects (see Chapter 3), but again the sessions were a valuable activity in and of themselves, acting as a tool to help us break out of preconceived ideas and habits.

Our brainstorming sessions adhered strictly to the rule that all ideas are valid and need to be captured. Our mantra during these sessions was "always say yes," that is, receive each and every idea openly and without prejudice or criticism. For some, it was tempting to express only ideas that seemed sensible or to evaluate others' ideas. We gradually discovered that the expression of outlandish ideas was a crucial part of the exercise. It was these seemingly off-the-wall ideas that helped us see beyond our routine ways of doing and thinking. Brainstorming allowed us to reframe our notions of what was possible and had an immediate effect of moving us beyond our preconceptions and preferences.

The structure of our brainstorming sessions varied but most included the following elements. One person acted as facilitator. At the beginning of the study, this role was most often filled by our resident anthropologist, but as time went on others began to act as facilitators. The facilitator's role was to explain the purpose and structure of the session, encourage the "always say yes" rule, promote a creative atmosphere, and make sure that there was a mechanism for capturing the ideas generated. In some cases, the brainstorming sessions started with a warm-up activity—something fun and outside our routine to put participants in a relaxed and creative mood.

The brainstorming itself took a variety of forms. In a large group, we might throw out ideas and have one person record them on a white board or a flipchart. As an alternative, we might have people spend five or ten minutes quietly jotting down their own ideas on sticky notes and then pass these on to others, who might generate related ideas. Other times we broke up into small groups to generate ideas verbally, jotting down one idea per sticky note and then regrouping as a whole to sort the ideas by category.

One participant reported that the brainstorming sessions were useful because "it is so easy to get into a rut about certain issues, and it can be very hard to get out of that rut." For her, brainstorming freed up her own train of thought, since she did not have "to think it through," and it allowed her to "really think off her feet." From her perspective, this helped open everyone's thought processes. The collective aspect of brainstorming was equally important in that it generated many more ideas than if each of us had done it alone.

Being Involved in the Study: The Experience of Staff Members

In this section, we report on the informal interviews conducted with twelve of the library staff members who took part in the study as well as on our own experiences as participants. We were interested in learning what it was like to be involved in the study and how participation affected the way we approached our work, students, and the mission of the library. Interviews were conducted in person or by telephone and included some version of the following questions:

- How were you involved in the Undergraduate Research Project, and what was your experience of being involved?
- What did you learn about undergraduates that surprised you?
- How has your understanding or perception of the students changed?
- Are there any ways your interactions with students or your daily tasks have changed?
- Has the Undergraduate Research Project affected your work in any way?

In general, each of the library staff we spoke with learned something new about the students. In some cases, staff perceptions of undergraduate life were reinforced by their involvement in the study. In other cases, beliefs were altered and viewpoints changed more dramatically.

Personal Benefits

Many participants felt that one of the most important benefits of the study was the optimism it generated. For example, several staff members talked about how enjoyable and interesting it was to be involved in the study. One staff member reported that the best thing about the project was learning ethnographic methods and being intellectually stimulated. Another librarian said that "one of the most wonderful things was to be involved in research again." Another staff member, whose job responsibilities involve few interactions with students, said that being involved in the project was a "good exercise for your mind and body." Her involvement helped her to not "get mired in the day-to-day" and made her work "more engaging." In addition, several staff talked about how the project gave them more confidence. For one librarian, the research increased his credibility with faculty members. This led directly to his regular attendance in an undergraduate class and to more interactions with students in the library.

In some cases, what we learned was not new, but it deepened our understanding. For example, several staff members explained that, even if a particular finding was not new, they had a greater depth of understanding about the issue from the students' perspective. It was a gut level feeling of "I really get it now." For example, one librarian described how powerful it was to watch video clips of students in their dorm rooms. She felt that watching these clips presented the students more fully and gave her a real picture of how the students are "not the same as we are."

For some staff, this deeper level of awareness created a greater comfort level with students. One staff member felt she had gained an increased understanding of undergraduates as well as increased confidence in students' ability to use the library and do research. One library staff member reported that she now thinks of undergraduates as individuals rather than as a group. In some cases, staff felt reassured that the strategies they were using to help and engage students actually worked.

This new level of understanding created apprehensions as well. As one staff member put it, the project acted as a "wake-up call," drawing attention to the amount of work that still needs to be done to prove our credibility to students and faculty. Motivated either by confidence or by apprehensions, several staff used their new insights to experiment with new approaches in their work with students.

Interacting with Students: At the Reference Desk and Beyond

Many participants noted small but important changes in their one-to-one interactions with students. For a few others, participation radically transformed their interactions with undergraduates. The project also offered an opportunity to renew and refresh interviewing and observation skills learned in graduate library degree programs.

From this new perspective, earlier interactions with students now appeared to be somewhat one-dimensional, with the stress on the librarian telling students how to find or do things. Now, interactions with students resemble something more like two-way conversations, or what one librarian called "a more level relationship."

In addition, specific findings of the study gave librarians a clearer understanding of how students work and provided a basis for starting or directing conversations. For example, our research taught us about the important role parents play in many students' lives. Thus, if a student is struggling with a topic, a librarian might ask, "Have you talked with anyone about your research?" The student's response, about parents or instructors, might then add more context and background to the discussion. We also learned how busy our students' lives are, such that they may work on a paper for several hours and then not pick it up for another two weeks. In this case, a reference librarian might ask a student, "Will you be working on this paper tonight? If so, you can definitely get back to us, we'll be here until nine tonight" In both of these examples, a deeper understanding of our students' academic and social practices led to interactions that were more comfortable and more attuned to students' needs.

One librarian reported that now she does not try to give the same "ideal" response to reference questions from undergraduates but instead focuses more on getting the context of the question right. Participation in the study reminded her how important it is to understand faculty expectations and to determine where the student is in the research and writing process. In general, her approach became less idealized but more practical, observing that students have more difficulty narrowing their topic and with writing itself, rather than with research-related problems.

Another librarian observed that she no longer agonizes over getting the students to come to the reference desk or approach a librarian. She recognizes that students want to work independently and was surprised at their level of confidence in their ability to find things, noting that we need to design Web pages and interfaces so that students can do what they need to do on their own. Now her strategy at the desk is not to bury students with suggestions but to get them started and let them know that they can come back for more help.

For some librarians, the study also enabled easier interaction with students away from the reference desk. Some reported that, when encountering a student in the elevator or approaching one in the book stacks, the conversation felt "more reciprocal." For others it meant being more careful and sensitive when conversing with students and having a fuller appreciation of the differences between individuals. In this way, the anthropological methods we practiced were useful beyond the official study, helping us create an easier rapport with our students.

Similarly, one staff member changed her individual training sessions with the student workers she supervised, based on her experience with the project. Previously she had relied on her own explanation of tasks and on instructional handouts. After being exposed to this generation of students' approaches to learning, she now finds it more effective to train students by "working alongside them." After talking her trainee through a procedure, she now has the student do it alone and encourages more questions. She says that she now takes time to "feel out" the student's perspective and then tailors her training accordingly. In this case, participation in the study inspired her to experiment with new student-centered teaching strategies.

Classroom Instructional Strategies

As a consequence of this project, several librarians have altered their instructional strategies. Some have made their instruction sessions more hands-on, wanting to emphasize two-way conversations. One librarian described a "more minimalist" approach to instruction. Though she is aware that students will likely encounter obstacles, she has learned that it is not helpful to convey all the complexities of the research process up front. Instead she supplies clues to get students started and then allows them to discover the richness of the research process on their own. Some librarians reported that they now spend more time observing their students in a hands-on classroom situation and sharing search tips relevant to their immediate needs.

In other instances, involvement in the study has led librarians to add to or reorient their classroom presentations. For example, the study taught us that many students do not understand what academic librarians do. As one person put it, "In the minds of students, librarians equal print." In response, some librarians report that they have added a sentence or two about the role of the librarian, telling the class, for example, that "a librarian can save you time." For example, instead of talking about the power of the search tips—a topic of great interest to librarians—she now relates concepts directly to what we know is important to our students: their need to be efficient with their time.

Other library staff have begun to use slightly different strategies to connect with students. For example, the study gave us a deeper understanding of how students interact with computer and communications technologies. This has allowed some staff to talk more effectively about how library tools relate to the students' existing knowledge of online searching. One staff member tells her students, "If what you find in Google isn't enough for your assignment, try this." Another librarian, again with students' busy schedules in mind, gives her class explicit after-hour time slots when she will be available at the reference desk. In both of these examples, librarians could have viewed students' use of Google or their inability to seek us out at the reference desk as points of frustration or barriers between students and librarians. But, with a better appreciation for why students do what they do, these librarians saw both of these issues not as barriers but as an opportunities.

Collaboration

The Undergraduate Research Project facilitated collaborative relationships among the library staff and helped the staff pursue the mission of the library more creatively. In fact, one staff member said that the greatest benefit of the study, more than any set of findings, was how it motivated staff. In addition, many staff enjoyed and benefited from working with other people in the library whom they had not previously known well. One staff member said that it was especially helpful to get to know other staff members for an extended period of time and "not as a one-shot deal." This collaborative atmosphere was also fostered by the research and ethnographic aspects of the project. A focus on doing research created a wonderfully neutral, exploratory environment. We learned that all of us, regardless of department or job description, had this in common: we did not know what our students are really like.

Discovering this common denominator led to fruitful discussions among staff and helped us transcend recurring debates, such as those about database interfaces. For example, one staff member reflected on how staff used to debate, again and again, whether we should have a simple search interface or a more complex interface. Being involved in the study helped all of us realize that, as far as our students were concerned, we did not really know what was best. By the end of the study, many of us had an expanded view of this issue, regardless of what

our original opinion might have been. In this particular case, a deeper understanding of the issues helped us see the value of both sides of this debate. As we learned more about our students, it became clear that we needed both simple and complex interfaces; we can now focus our energies on the interactions of both. One library staff member observed that we now respond differently, both as a group and individually, at vendor database demonstrations: "We are able to give constructive feedback from the point of view of the student. We put ourselves in the shoes of the students."

As discussed throughout this chapter, participation in the project encouraged staff to experiment with new ideas and techniques. Because this took place within the context of research, the experimentation seemed less threatening. Participants were not engaged in making library-wide policy decisions or working in committees to solve problems. Instead, the study created, as one librarian put it, a comfort level with "hit or miss" and with different people trying different things. Instead of agonizing over getting it right, innovation was happening on a grassroots level.

In addition, by focusing so intently on our students, the project helped orient us, as a staff, toward our mission for students. One staff member remarked that the project had an interesting parallel to the idea of strategic planning, except that instead of looking inward toward ourselves we were looking outward toward our students. When debates about issues arise now, we have a common language and shared understanding about students. This has meant that we are better prepared to meet new challenges and to move forward as a library.

Thoughts for Future Projects

Even though the staff felt very positive about the project, it is worth considering what we might do differently in the future. As discussed earlier, a large number of staff members participated. We later discovered, though, that additional staff had wanted to be involved. This was a natural progression of the project; as more staff learned about the study, interest grew. In retrospect, however, there are some simple ways to make future projects more inclusive. For example, the lunch hour coviewing sessions were inconvenient for some staff. The timing of these sessions could have easily varied: lunch, mid-afternoon, and mid-morning. In addition, the reference-sponsored coviewing sessions were advertised only to subject librarians. It would have been interesting to advertise at least some of these meetings to the entire library staff.

In addition, several staff members have expressed an interest in continuing the project. We are aware of how easy it is to fall back into our old habits and typical frustrations with students and to lose the collaborative and experimental mood created by the study. But what is the best way to proceed? And how do we not lose the rich environment that ethnographic research has given us? One idea was to sponsor a regularly scheduled brown-bag lunch or mid-afternoon "snack break." During this one-hour discussion, hosted on a rotating basis by a staff member who participated in the study, we examine a topic of current interest to public services through the lens of what we learned during the Undergraduate Research Project. We also continue to collect and analyze data on a limited basis.

Another idea is to sponsor more research-inspired implementations. This allows us to try small experiments on a preliminary basis, with the focus on what we can learn with small investments of time and resources. In addition, staff now trained in some ethnographic methods are equipped to conduct mini-studies. For example, a small group of staff may form an ad hoc team to interview a few students about a particular issue.

In late 2006, the River Campus Libraries began a two-year research project on graduate students. With generous funding from the Institute of Museum and Library Services, we will delve into the academic practices of graduate students, with a particular focus on the research and authoring of dissertations, using many of the methodologies that proved so successful in our undergraduate project.

Regardless of what approaches we pursue, our staff are strongly committed to nurturing the benefits derived thus far from the Undergraduate Research Project and to striving to broaden them.

Note

1. We had permission from all of the students involved in the study to share interview content with library staff. In addition, in order to err on the side of caution, we regularly reminded those who attended coviewing sessions to keep the identities of the students anonymous and, when later conversing with others, to talk in more general terms and not in regards to specific students.

nine. Then and Now: How Today's Students Differ

Sarada George

As the Undergraduate Research Project progressed, we began to see how our current students' study and research practices differ from our own activities as students, especially in relation to technology use. When most of our library staff were in college, we had stereo systems, electric typewriters, dorm phones, office copiers, and sometimes televisions at school. Our students, in contrast, take a wide range of digital technology for granted as a normal part of their lives and use computer hardware and software that allow them to be connected constantly to each other, their families, their friends, and an almost infinite amount of information. This connection is so ubiquitous in their lives that, even though they use this technology everywhere and almost all the time, some of them feel the need to escape from it on occasion, especially to concentrate on difficult academic work.

Who are these new students, who are so different from today's librarians and library assistants? How long and how fast had these changes been going on under our noses while we looked the other way? For us, one obvious place to turn was to the literature, which informed us that our students today are part of a generation often called the Millennials (Howe and Strauss 2003). Many descriptions of the Millennials fit the findings of our Undergraduate Research Project. But before exploring these comparisons, I review the literature on the generations of students who preceded the Millennial.

Generational Groups

By the mid-twentieth century, it became clear that the pace of technological change was greater than ever before in human history; there was every reason to believe the trend would continue and escalate (Toffler 1970). Today's young people and college students are seeing a vastly different world from the one their grandparents, parents, and even most of their academic librarians knew in their own college years. Each group of freshmen arriving on college campuses comes with a different worldview, a different set of assumptions about the world, based on the general and specific situations they grew up with and the environment they saw around them (Beloit College 2006). What you take for granted as normal and ordinary depends on what already exists in your world when you arrive on the scene (Greenfield 2006). Differences in these assumptions can result in perceived "generation gaps"—attitudinal disconnects and misunderstandings between age cohorts. According to Twenge (2006), a person's cultural experiences, expectations, assumptions, and worldview are determined at least as much by his/her time period (and therefore generation) as by family and personal circumstances.

Although there is some disagreement on the birthyear endpoints that should be used in defining generations, there seems to be a broad consensus on the idea of generational comparisons and on some basic characteristics of each group. As of the beginning of the twenty-first

Sarada George is Library Assistant at the River Campus Libraries, University of Rochester; e-mail: sgeorge@library. rochester.edu.

century, the population of living Americans can be divided into six generations (Mitchell 2000; Howe and Strauss 2003; Oblinger 2003). Leaving out the small surviving numbers who reached adulthood before the era of World War II, there are five American generations with different overall characters. All five groups are represented on college campuses today and have to interact with each other to some extent.

The *World War II Generation* (or GI, or Greatest Generation) consists of men and women who were old enough to have fought or participated in World War II, whether or not they actually did so. They had unprecedented access to higher education as a result of the G.I. Bill but are still less educated, on the whole, than subsequent groups. They experienced the Great Depression and the creation of suburbia in the United States. They were accustomed to teamwork and achievement and were oriented toward community action within the system (Howe and Strauss 2003).

The next group, called the *Silent Generation* (or Swing Generation), was born late enough not to have been of age during the war; they were either children or babies during wartime. Sandwiched between the influential generations that came before and after them, and smaller in numbers, they spent their formative years in a prosperous, socially and economically quiet period after World War II (Mitchell 2000).

The parents of most of today's college students are part of the *Baby Boom Generation* (often called simply Boomers). Born from the end of World War II through the 1950s and early 1960s, they are currently still the largest cohort in American history (Mitchell 2000), though they are likely to be passed in size by their children's generation (Howe and Strauss 2003). This group is the first to be raised with television as a pervasive part of their lives (Twenge 2006) and is associated with anti-authoritar-

ian, countercultural attitudes and behavior (Mitchell 2000). As children or young adults, they lived through the cold war, space race, civil rights movement, sexual revolution, feminist movement, Vietnam War, and Watergate.

Many of the librarians serving current college students fall into the Baby Boom Generation. As of 2005, sixty-five percent of academic librarians were age 45 or older (Wilder 2005). This is the typical age group of parents of college students, so the contrasts between Boomers and Millennials affect students' interactions in their libraries as well as at home. These differences are even likely to increase over time, following a trend in the distribution of librarian ages, which is shifting upward (Wilder 2003).

Generation X (or the Baby Bust, or Latchkey Generation) spans birth years from the mid-1960s through the 1970s, with various authors using different endpoints (Howe and Strauss 2003; Oblinger 2003; Oblinger and Oblinger 2005). Occasionally referred to as a "slacker" cohort, this generation is the first to have computers as a central part of their lives. They have been influenced by the fall of the Berlin Wall and communism in Europe, the rise of the Internet and World Wide Web, the AIDS epidemic, Tiananmen Square, Chernobyl, and the Challenger disaster.

The children of the Boomers are often called the *Millennials* (or Generation Y, the Net Generation, the Echo Boom, Gen Next, or the Baby Boomlet) and were born, according to different points of view, starting in the late 1970s or early 1980s and continuing to the 1990s or, possibly, as far as the present (Howe and Strauss 2003). These students do not have any real memories of the cold war or the Soviet Union, have almost never used postal mail, and have grown up with Google, barcodes, DNA fingerprinting, instant messaging, and reality TV (Oblinger 2003; Beloit College 2006).

Studies of Previous Generations

Recent students have been studied, or at least discussed, fairly extensively; in fact, reports on the characteristics of the Millennials appear with startling frequency in the national media. At the University of Rochester, it was evident to us that students had changed, but it was not clear what the changes were. To get a clear picture of the differences, we must first look at the students of previous generations.

Foley and Foley (1969) conducted numerous interviews with students in the late 1960s as part of the College Poll and noticed similarities, as well as great differences, over time. They note that in the early twentieth century college students came primarily from the social elite, and consequently the college population was small, lacking in diversity, and mostly male. In 1962 only a third of college students were female (Sanford 1962), whereas women today tend to be a majority on campus (Twenge 2006). The atmosphere or student culture at many colleges a hundred years ago was much like an exclusive club.

As higher education became increasingly necessary for entry into careers and as financial aid entered into the equation, the college population became more diverse. Current undergraduate students are the first truly global generation in the United States, with greater diversity in race and ethnicity than any previous generation (Howe and Strauss 2003). One-fifth of them have at least one parent who immigrated from elsewhere.

American college student culture has changed regularly, almost by the decade, in the past century (Moffatt 1989), with members of each generation rebelling against and attempting to correct what they saw as the most egregious trends of the immediately prior generations and perhaps, in some important respects, ultimately resembling their grandparents more than their parents (Howe and Strauss 2003).

Sanford (1962) found that Vassar students in the 1960s differed significantly from those of the 1950s, who perceived their world as socially and economically stable and accepted authority without confrontation. What changed in the interval was the development of an international "youth culture" without social class or national boundaries (Moffatt 1989). After this youth "revolution" in the 1960s, there were fewer differences than before between young people on and off college campuses.

Several changes have had large, transformative effects, altering the nature of higher education for all future students—like a "continental divide" in the history of higher education. One such divide, previously mentioned, was the opening up of colleges to less affluent students after World War II. Another was the renunciation by colleges of their role *in loco parentis* (the substitute parent role), which occurred in the late 1960s. This, along with the international youth culture, had a profound effect on college students, beginning with the Baby Boomers (Moffatt 1989), who had a generation gap in communicating with their parents and other older authority figures. The differences between the Millennials and those before them may be evidence of a third major divide.

University of Rochester Students

At the University of Rochester, we have observed several important student characteristics that the literature attributes to the Millennial generation and that set them apart from earlier generations.

Parent–Child Relationship

Our students seem to be much more in touch with their parents than in previous generations, including their parents' own cohort. The University of Rochester students we studied mentioned a great deal of communication with their parents as well as parental involvement in their research papers, such as in the search for a topic or in proofreading drafts. Several mentioned communicating with their parents via instant messaging. Clearly, and somewhat to our surprise, these students maintain quite close ties back home. There is even a specifically named "Hi, Mom balcony" in the student union at the University of Rochester from which students can wave to a parent through a Web cam.[1] Baby Boomers could never have had such close contact with their parents, even if they had wanted to.

The Baby Boom parents seem to be sheltering their children more than they themselves were sheltered. This may derive partly from American culture's attitudes toward children, which changed noticeably in the 1970s, focusing on children in several ways and becoming more obsessed with child safety (Howe and Strauss 2003). Today's students grew up in an era of metal scanners in schools, transparent backpacks, and multiplying government regulations for their protection. At a time when terrorism, crime, privacy, and safety issues are constantly in the news, the Boomer parents of today's students raised them with more attention to the details of their lives than previous parents provided. Some Boomers even want colleges to return to *in loco parentis*. These attitudes have given rise to what is now referred to as the "helicopter parent," who hovers over a child's college experience, trying to exert as much control as possible and generally interfering in even the smallest details of the student's life. Today's students are even similar to their parents in their tastes in music and clothing, and they are generally closer to their parents, experiencing less of a generation gap than any other group studied on this issue (Howe and Strauss 2003; Twenge 2006).

Communication

The current college environment may be most visibly different from the past in the vastly increased use of digital technology. This is turning out to be the source of the latest major divide in higher education, with effects at least as pervasive as those of financial aid, the international youth culture, and the renunciation of in *loco parentis*. New and ever-changing technologies are more integrated into the academic and social lives of today's students than they were in those of earlier generations. For the grandparents of today's college students, radio was the most characteristic and pervasive technology; our students' parents watched television, and they themselves use the Internet (McMillan and Morrison 2006). Millennials are not just users of the new technologies, they are "digital natives" who grew up and are comfortable functioning in this technological world (Prensky 2001).

There are a multitude of portable gadgets available to students now, such as laptop computers, BlackBerry-type hand-held devices, MP3 players, and cell phones. Nationally, most college students tote around at least one of these and may have used cell phones for several years already. The types of electronic media currently available for use in homes and dormitories, and the ways they can be used to connect with people and other media, have become increasingly complex in the past thirty years (Lomas and Oblinger 2006).

Locally, a 2005 survey conducted as part of the Undergraduate Research Project found that cell phones are an extremely common portable communications technology, and the one students would choose if they could have only one. All the freshmen surveyed had a cell phone, as did 93 percent of the upperclassmen. This ratio has exploded in the past several years. For example, in 2001 only one circulation desk student employee at the science and engineering library listed a cell phone number, but by fall semester 2006, cell phones were listed exclusively by all of the student employees. Moreover, the students tend not even to know the number of their dorm room phone, since they never use it. This trend will only increase over time, especially as cell phones become more sophisticated by supporting multiple uses, including social networking, Web browsing, and global positioning. Students expect to be able to be connected—to the Internet, to their friends, families, and fellow students—at any time, from anywhere (Rainie 2006).

Our Rochester students are constantly in touch with their large groups of friends, through physical and electronic means. Several of them particularly mentioned their study groups as well as a "study buddy," someone they regularly study with, who may or may not be in any of the same classes. In many classes, academic work is structured to allow team presentations and studying, and even grading is sometimes in group terms. Not all of this is very different from the habits of their parents' generation, some of whom also remember studying in groups, but it accords with the findings of several authors who describe Millennials as being oriented toward a peer group dynamic (Howe and Strauss 2006; Greenfield 2006; Rainie 2006).

Having grown up in the current high-tech world, today's students expect to be able to communicate instantly with anyone, anywhere in the world (Alch 2000). Online social networking tools allow young people to have large groups of friends, all electronically connected with each other much of the time (Thomas and McDonald 2005). They are connected to this electronic world almost constantly (Lomas and Oblinger 2006). According to our informal surveys, the vast majority of University of Rochester students make regular use of Facebook and similar social networking websites. Students use Facebook and similar online services that specialize in interpersonal connections on a daily basis to meet new people, connect with their real-life friends, and even create

study groups by finding students in the same course (Read 2004).

The Multitasking Approach

In this electronically connected environment, many different kinds of tasks can be performed from the same location, and the same task can be done in different locations. Students frequently do several things, often completely unrelated, at the same time. For example, here is an exchange between one of our project team members and an undergraduate student who is working on a computer science lab assignment:

> **Interviewer:** "Are you playing poker at the same time?"
>
> **Student:** "Ahh, yeah."
>
> **Interviewer:** "You have a hand open. Oh, you have two hands open."
>
> **Student:** "Actually, I think I have five."

These five poker hands are all being played at the same time as the student is working on the computer assignment. He sees nothing unusual in being online with other people while doing academic work.

This habit of multitasking is seen as an important characteristic of Millennials (Howe and Strauss 2003; Greenfield 2006). Taubenek (2006) reports, "They will have a laptop in front of them and iPod headphones on while they are typing something and checking IMs all up and down one side of the screen." These students are firmly convinced that they can learn properly while doing several other things at the same time, such as listening to music (McGlynn 2005). This is such an important part of their lives that they may even think differently from previous generations; Greenfield (2006) refers to Millennials as having "hyperlinked minds"—they jump from one connection to another rather than follow a linear progression.

Not all Millennials are comfortable multitasking in every aspect of their work. Attempting to perform several tasks simultaneously may sometimes distract them from academic work. One student in our project, talking about using e-mail, said, "Yeah, that's why I go to the library. So I do not have my computer and actually do work." Some students at the University of Rochester indicated that, at least when working on research papers, they tend to work in spurts. They may go for a period of weeks without working on the paper at all, but when it becomes necessary to focus on it (usually because some other interim step or the finished paper is due) they may work on it to the exclusion of most other activities for hours at a stretch. Several students said they prefer to write their papers in environments of relative solitude, avoiding electronic distractions. This seems to indicate that multitasking does not work for these students all the time. When deep concentration is required, some of them seem, like generations of students before them, to need to work on one task at a time, and even to find quiet places in which to do it.

Perhaps Millennials are not as universally different from earlier students as some current research suggests. Though they use the new digital technology heavily, perhaps it does not define their lives as much as redefine the way they relate to the various locations in which they spend their day. Cell phones, wireless networks, and other technological developments have freed today's students from some of the physical constraints that limited earlier generations.

The Use of Physical Space

A primary difference in the way Millennials function in the academic world is that they prefer to learn anywhere they may be, in social settings as well as academic, using digital technology in ways that suit them individually. This means that learning does not take place only or even primarily in classrooms or study spaces; anywhere students congregate is a venue for academic work, a coffee shop is just as likely as a dorm room or lounge (Lomas and Oblinger 2006). Students want to customize their own ways of learning and will use whatever is available, often in ways not envisioned by the creators of the technology. For example, students physically present on college campuses use distance-learning tools as often as the off-campus and out-of-town students for whom these tools were originally intended (Carlson 2005).

Students have some very definite ideas of what they would like to have available to support their individual ways of studying. When the undergraduate project's digital subteam asked a group of students to design an ideal library website, the results were imaginative (see Chapter 5). The student designers wanted connections from one site to everything a student would ever need to use, from course reserves, databases, instant messaging, and e-mail to their own personal schedules and a way to order pizza. When other students were asked to design their ideal physical library space, they wanted group study areas and public spaces as well as quiet study areas, food and coffee service, and even places to take naps (see Chapter 4). They want a great deal to be available to them, possibly because they are trying to get a great deal done, all the time.

Students at the University of Rochester seem to be constantly busy; the mapping diaries they made of their movements during a full day show that they are on the go nearly all the time (see Chapter 7). They often depend on day planners—electronic or paper—to keep track of their activities. One of our students explicitly characterized college life as being "always on the run." The literature shows that Millennials have been heavily scheduled from early childhood and are a more pressured generation than any other (Howe and Strauss 2003; Taubenek 2006). In general, their lives have always been overplanned, with much less unstructured time than youngsters twenty or thirty years before them (Howe and Strauss 2003). College students eat irregularly and have little free time, even to sleep. Most of the students we interviewed do more of their sustained studying and academic work in the evening and late at night rather than during the day, when they are occupied mostly with classes, labs, recitations, jobs, and group meetings. Often students are away from their dorm rooms for most of the day and do academic work only when they return. One student said, "When I get back to my room for the day at like ten or whenever, I will sit down and do my work then." According to one interviewee, "You don't get serious until after dinner, usually," and this appears to be a common pattern.

Dormitories tend to be noisy and may not always be the best places for the concentrated bouts of academic work. Our students use the library primarily for studying, often going to the same spots repeatedly. Several indicated that they went there in order to avoid the distractions of electronic communication devices. One student, commenting on using instant messaging while studying in the library, said, "It gets distracting so I try not to. I'll put up an away message or I'll just completely turn it off." That particular student studies in the book stacks area, but many others prefer more comfortable seating. In our design study, where students envisioned their ideal library environment, comfortable, relaxing spaces were always included (see Chapter 4).

In needing such spaces, today's students may not be much different from other generations, but their use of the space and what they are escaping from may demonstrate some differences. This may be the first generation that comes to the library to escape from communication. Many often do not even bring their laptops with them, usually "because it weighs a ton." Instead they use computers in the campus computing centers or library study areas when they are away from their dorm rooms. The need for comfortable spaces in which to relax and unwind at all hours of the day and night has been noticed by other researchers as well (Howe and Strauss 2003) and can probably be attributed to a desire to escape the constant pressure and connectedness of student life.

Emerging Trends: A Technology Backlash?

Some of the students in our project needed a partial escape from computer technology itself, preferring, for example, to print out articles to read for a paper or print a paper draft to proofread rather than doing it entirely on the computer. One student who had just written a paper said she always proofreads from a printout: "I print it out, I can't read it on screen. I don't know; my eyes just don't work that way." These occasional retreats from computer technology came up periodically in our interviews and were slightly surprising. It is hard to tell whether technological improvements will change things like this or whether some students will continue to prefer to read paper materials. This is important to keep in mind as we attempt to follow wherever the latest technology leads.

The literature also mentions some downsides to constant electronic connectedness, including the distractions some of our students brought up. Electronic communication and social networking tools can be a means of procrastination (Taubenek 2006) and can even lead to what has been identified as Internet addiction (McMillan and Morrison 2006). Those who do carry laptops around do not get better grades than others, but they do spend more time on Web surfing, instant messaging, and other nonacademic activities (Read 2006). Colleges are responding in different ways to these problems. Some professors are already refusing to allow laptops in class on the grounds that they are too much of a distraction from the lecture, and in some classrooms Internet connectivity can be switched on or off at the professor's discretion (Young 2006). Lower grade point averages have also been found to correlate with more playing of computer games; though students feel they have the technological skills they need for academics, they do not always seem to have equivalent levels of problem-solving skills (Oblinger and Oblinger 2005).

In fact, students may not be quite the digital technology experts their elders assume they are. They prefer instant messaging to e-mail and offhandedly use cell phone text messaging, blogs, and wikis (Greenfield 2006). But even those students with high levels of technological skill may not necessarily have adequate communication skills in general. They may not have the listening skills or attention spans of earlier generations. They do not read as much as their predecessors (Carlson 2005). Though Millennials want to be able to choose how they learn (McGlynn 2005), they may not function as well as previous generations in terms of independent thinking (Carlson 2005). Though they are comfortable with the new technology, they are not necessarily good at using the information it brings them (Thomas and McDonald 2005). These are clearly issues librarians need to address. Our study shows, however, that this will not be as simple as one might hope. One of the reasons our students are not likely to consult librarians in their research is that they already have a great deal of confidence in their ability to do it on their own (see Chapter 2).

This confidence may be a result of the focus on children in the past several decades and the heavy emphasis on the teaching of self-esteem in school. When 66,000 college students were tested on a measure of self-esteem over several decades, male students in the 1990s tested 86 percent higher, and females 71 percent higher, than those in the 1960s. The later students had high expectations for their own success, sometimes in stark contrast with the reality of their talents and opportunities (Twenge 2006). We found our University of Rochester students to be confident in their abilities to find and evaluate information and to obtain the course grades they wanted.

Today's students are pragmatic and focused on their future careers, viewing their education and other aspects of their lives primarily as means to reach their career goals (Nathan 2005). Many of the students we interviewed had fairly clear ideas about what they wanted to do, what courses and grades would be necessary to succeed, and their ability to attain them. They and their Boomer parents have high standards for a college's responsibility for the safety and success of students, and the children have high expectations of adults with whom they have contact (Howe and Strauss 2003). It is somewhat surprising in this context that these expectations do not seem to extend to the staff of campus libraries. Our students expect technology of every sort to work properly at all times and to be able to access everything they need, but they do not, as a rule, think to come to the reference desk and demand our assistance.

We wondered what would happen if we tried to make use of instant messaging to reach students, but our brief experiment found no evidence that undergraduates would use this tool to contact library reference desks. This could change, however, over a longer period and with more publicity. There is evidence in the literature (Roper and Kindred 2005) that students will use instant messaging to contact professors who make themselves available that way to complement in-person office hours. It is premature to draw conclusions at this point, though. Many of our students seemed to be telling us that in-person communication is still of primary importance to them. One student said, "I would say the closer my relationship is with a person, the more I feel comfortable talking to them online. But at the same time, the more I see them … face-to-face." Lomas and Oblinger (2006) also found that communication technology could not substitute for real connections with other people.

Conclusion

The college campus of the twenty-first century has not really been an ivory tower for many years now. It is caught up in the general headlong rush toward ever-greater technological sophistication. The students on campus now have grown up accustomed to high levels of computer technology and are impatient with many aspects of higher education that have not yet adapted, the library included. Though they are not all Millennials chronologically, they and their universities must learn to adjust to the Millennials and their even more digital successors, who will be shaping the colleges of this century.

These students may appear like a new breed to those who staff the libraries and were students decades before. Today's students are prepared to make high demands on their schools. Though their attention may be more fragmented than was usual in the past, these students believe that academically they are doing very well. And, for the most part, at least as far as we have seen in our Undergraduate Research Project, they are. But although Millennials cannot avoid being molded to a great degree by the technologies and attitudes of the present, academic libraries are only just beginning to make the necessary adjustments.

Note

1. http://www.rochester.edu/aboutus/wilsonwebcam.html.

ten. The Mommy Model of Service

Nancy Fried Foster

In this chapter, I focus on a few specific trends in the Undergraduate Research Project data that relate to service in general, and to reference outreach in particular, and draw some general conclusions about students and their library use. I write as an anthropologist, and as the person on the project with the broadest responsibility for methodology and fieldwork.

Since the project began in the summer of 2004, I have asked many of the reference librarians who participated what they like best about their work as librarians as well as about their frustrations and the ways their roles have changed over the years. I have learned that many of these librarians started in their professional careers at a time when there was a different kind of demand for their services. They had a higher level of meaningful contact with library patrons; students thronged the desk and there were two reference librarians on duty. Now, a single librarian might languish at the desk for hours, only to be asked for directions to the restroom or to lend a patron a fork.

Of course, librarians are not really languishing at the desk. They are hard at work behind the scenes, making sure that the library does everything its users need it to do, such as allow them access to the full text of articles right on their computer screens, no matter where they may be. The new demands and opportunities of their work notwithstanding, many librarians have prepared themselves for a career helping students and faculty members track down hard-to-find information and can feel disappointed that they are less frequently called upon to use their well-honed reference skills.

But librarians have also been concerned with the scholarly mission of the library. Specifically, they have felt that students and other library users have not been making best use of library resources, instead consulting Google, Wikipedia, and other websites and services to answer their own questions, sometimes poorly, rather than finding warranted information in the libraries' scholarly collections. They also believe that patrons only scratch the surface of the collections and miss out on the richness of the holdings—the important but hard-to-find works, the rarities, the treasures, the historical and esoteric materials that they and their predecessors have lovingly collected, preserved, and cataloged for generations in the hopes of making them available to new cohorts of library users.

The reasons for studying undergraduates have been complex. One motivation has been the desire to figure out what it would take to get more students to come to the desk asking for help, to restore the face-to-face interactions and the opportunities to provide that special kind of service—caring and personalized, intellectually demanding, expert and informed—that attracted so many librarians to their field in the first place.

Nancy Fried Foster is Lead Anthropologist at the River Campus Libraries, University of Rochester; e-mail: nfoster@library.rochester.edu.

We came up with a research question designed to give us insight into student perspectives and experiences: What do students *really* do when they write their research papers? Librarians expected that if they had a better understanding of the student research and writing process, they could improve their interactions with students and help them find and use better scholarly and research materials, thereby enhancing the learning experience for more students. With this overarching research question, library staff have pursued several different research activities, including interviews, observations, map diaries—many of them described in this book.

For example, library staff undertook a reference desk survey to understand changing patterns at the reference desk and followed that up with a set of brief interviews in the student union (see Chapter 2). The survey and interviews revealed that few students understand what reference librarians do and how reference librarians can help them, nor do they consider asking for the help reference librarians are trained to provide. Rather, students tend to feel that they are good at finding their own resources and answering their own questions. If they need expert advice, they turn either to their instructors or, surprisingly, to their families, whom they contact by phone or e-mail.

Workshops in which students designed their ideal library spaces provided additional insight on reference outreach. As we saw in Chapter 4, most students simply leave reference librarians out of the picture. Interestingly, some put reference librarians at desks that also supply technical support, coffee, and office supplies and check out books. To a librarian, the circulation desk, reference desk, coffee cart, and IT help desk are clearly for different purposes and staffed by different kinds of experts, but many students do not recognize these distinctions.

Interviews of students who had written research papers added information about how students organize their research activities and integrate them into other everyday activities (see Chapter 8). Librarians have been struck by the degree to which students maintain contact with their families, asking their parents to edit their work and even to help them select their topics and find resources. They also find that students have a high opinion of their own ability to find resources and assume that, if they cannot find resources through the library's Web presence, it is because the library does not have them.

As the information has come in from these and other research activities, librarians have confronted the fact that students and librarians have vastly different orientations to the library. I believe that part of this difference has to do with a profound change in the nature of service over the past several decades. What follows is an attempt to describe the student view of library reference in the context of an overall student model of service. I contrast this model to the librarian's view and investigate the implications of these different views for the library and for understanding students.

Librarians' Models of Service

Reference librarians have a professional model of service, which they learn in library or information science programs, and which is evident in their professional practice. This model of service is clearly visible in the "reference interview." In its ideal form, this interaction requires that the librarian be approachable and interested in the needs of the patron, establishing eye contact and focusing attention on the patron, inquiring about the patron's needs and the strategies s/he has used so far, providing on-the-spot support for finding materials, and taking steps to ensure that the patron is fully served (Reference and Users Service Association 2007).

In addition to explicit, taught models of service, librarians also have a tacit and more general model of service, just like the average person, which goes well beyond the library. This is a more personal and unspoken model, and it has a strong influence on their behaviors and expectations. It is a model of service developed since childhood, and it derives from personal experiences of service, for example, in shops, gas stations, restaurants, offices, and bookstores.

The average academic librarian is white, female, well educated, and just under 50 years old (Wilder 2003); accordingly, an average librarian's tacit model of service would be familiar to any middle-class, well-educated, white woman who was born around 1956. At the time these librarians were 10 years old, in 1966, service was much more extensive and courteous than it is now. When their parents needed gas, an attendant filled the tank and washed the windshield. When they needed shoes, their mother might take them to a shoe store, where a shoe salesman measured their feet, fetched a few styles in their size from a storage area in the back of the store, and then helped them try these shoes on, making sure they fit properly.

If their parents needed a camera, a television, or a typewriter, they went to a camera store, a television store, or a typewriter store, or perhaps to a well-staffed department store, and got advice from a specialized salesperson. If that camera, television, or typewriter broke, it could be returned to the store for expert repairs.

If someone in the family got sick, the doctor might very well have made a house call—that was still done in those days, though the practice was already in decline. In 1966, if you wanted a book, you would probably have gone to your local booksellers. At that time, Barnes & Noble had only its original New York store; it did not start to turn into the large chain and online presence it is today until the 1970s (Barnes & Noble Booksellers n.d.). Borders Books did not exist; it was established as a used bookstore only in 1971 (Borders Group n.d.). Instead of today's megabookstores, the 1966 Rochester phone directory listed fourteen independent bookstores, places where salespeople could advise you on a purchase or find a special item for you.

In 1966, when the average librarian of today was 10 years old, the Rochester phone book listed 116 meat markets and ten milliners (hat makers). There were seventy-eight bakeries. The names of department stores took up two and one half columns. Specialization and personal attention prevailed twenty years after World War II and well into the Vietnam era. That was the milieu in which today's average librarians formed their ideas of service.

Students' Models of Service

As I write this chapter it is early 2007 and the average freshman at the University of Rochester was born in 1988. By the time these students entered school, "self-service" was such an established concept that it seemed as if people had always pumped their own gas and shopped in megadiscount stores or online emporia. Many of today's students are used to getting medical assistance from physician's assistants, nurse practitioners, medical reference books for home use, or even websites, and less often from doctors. They certainly do not expect a house call. But these are relatively recent developments. Though students feel comfortable with all of this, the typical librarian has had to learn this new model of service and may feel that it is not really service at all.

In 1998, when today's freshman was 10 years old, the Rochester yellow pages listed thirty-two meat markets, down from 116 in 1966. This number has since fallen to twenty-seven. There were sixty bakeries, down from seventy-eight; today, only forty-nine remain. By 1998 there were no custom milliners and only six retail hat stores, now down to four. The old department stores had already begun to close, replaced by KMarts and WalMarts; where there had been two and one half columns worth of department stores in 1966, by 1998 there was scarcely one, and this has shrunk even further now, with Target and Kohl's ascendant.

Borders Books established a branch in Rochester in the early 1990s, when today's freshmen at the University of Rochester were young children. Simultaneously, many of the local bookstores began closing their doors, so that now the vast majority of bookstores in Rochester sell only used books or pornography or specialize in Christian or New Age books. It seems completely natural to our students these days to go online to buy books, or almost anything. If they shop at "real" stores, the only service they expect is help in finding an item and completing the sale, if that. Now that self-checkout is available at many supermarkets and discount stores, it is possible to conduct an entire transaction without human contact. Given the change in the day-to-day service experience, it is hardly a surprise that today's students have a vastly different concept of service than librarians—or that they feel comfortable seeking answers to their questions on Wikipedia, WebMD, and Google. But there is more to the story than self-service gas stations and online medical help.

In 1966, when the average librarian was 10 years old, service was a relationship. It might be enduring or brief, or even a one-time relationship, but the give and take between the service provider and the client was important in itself. The service provider established his/her expertise and credentials while angling for business and loyalty. The client evaluated the service provider or vendor while disclosing his/her needs and angling for preferential treatment. This is not to say that these relationships were mere economic-rational transactions. They were what remained of client relationships histori-

cally embedded in face-to-face societies, in which everybody knew everybody and your neighbor was your butcher, or your doctor, or your pastor, or your seamstress, or even your librarian.

The world has changed for librarians and students alike. Few service situations allow for the development of an interpersonal relationship, no matter how brief. Most butchers now work nowhere near the customers, whether in the back of a large supermarket or in an offsite processing facility. The same is true of bank tellers and the order fulfillment personnel who work in warehouses, assembling the books in an Amazon.com order or the apparel in a Lands' End order. Even librarians fall into this category, when you consider all they do on the digital side. And, of course, real people program Google and maintain it and improve it. But in these situations there is hardly a relationship at all; there is scarcely any person-to-person interaction.

The student model of service is self-service. Of course, it really only looks like self-service, depending as it does on real people working in backrooms. But looking at it from the student's end, it often entails running down a tacit list of self-service strategies until one works. When students talk about the actions they take to find books and articles for their research papers, many of them communicate an overall strategy of finding just enough, as quickly as possible, and then stopping. They start with the instructor's recommendations, move quickly to the online library catalog, and then on to Google, consulting Wikipedia and unwarranted websites for tips and shortcuts. Fortunately, this is not true of all students, but it is common enough in the data that we recognize it as a significant trend.

It is tempting to relate this trend to lack of time, but I think it resembles a pattern of information seeking that is evident in students' recreational activities—gaming, for example—when time is not an issue. Video and computer games come with little by way of directions. Manuals are available but not all gamers want or use them. When a gamer gets stuck in a game, s/he commonly runs through a variety of information-seeking activities, starting with experimentation with the game itself (Gee 2003). If this fails, the gamer may seek an online site for the particular game to see whether there are any "tips" or "tricks" that solve the problem. The point is that the parsimony of the gamers' information seeking is not related to time pressure. It is related to a view of life in which instrumentality trumps relationship.

So self-service is the preeminent model and strategy of the information-seeking student. But when the student cannot satisfy his/her own needs and turns to real-life service providers, what happens? In their drawings of ideal library spaces, students sometimes group librarians with technical support staff and baristas at service desks (see Chapter 4). When they do not differentiate between different kinds of service providers, it is in part because they do not know the service providers, having experienced few person-to-person service relationships. If they have a need, they want it filled. If they want a need filled, they want to go to a font of all sorts of service, a sort of universal service point, a physical Google. In other words, they want Mommy. And indeed, in many student narratives of the paper-writing process, family members figure importantly as providers of advice, resources, and editing services. Many students stay in close touch with their families, talking on the phone with their parents and exchanging e-mail and instant messages (Gardner 2007; see also Chapter 9). And we should note that it is not only students who want access to the font of all good things. Library staff enjoy all the benefits of new technologies, even while they mourn the loss of full service. And the same can be said of faculty.

It may seem contradictory to say that students want self-service because it fits their instrumental, non-relationship view of the world and then say that they want Mommy. Isn't Mommy everyone's first and most intense relationship? But "Mommy" is not the same as a real student's real mother, a person with whom s/he has a complex and ever-changing, ever-maturing relationship. When I speak of the Mommy Model of Service, I refer to a Mommy who is the provider of everything to the infant.

Implications of the Mommy Model of Service for the Library

If students want either to take care of themselves or have "Mommy" help them, what does that mean for the library? One thing it means is that there are many students who are very good at learning about and locating traditional and digital materials from varied sources with a wide range of finding aids. They take care of themselves very well. In this, many of them follow the model of their professors, and others take advantage of bibliographic instruction or online help, or just use the library's Web presence until they understand it. Research shows that heavy users of traditional resources tend also to be heavy users of electronic resources (Abbott 2006). If the library can provide these skilled and heavy users with even better tools, the use of both physical and digital collections will increase.

Understanding the student point of view makes it possible for library staff to see how things look to students. For example, librarians understand the difference between the various service points in the library and on campus. However, our research shows that students do not necessarily know that reference and circulation are two different desks, designed for different purposes. They expect that anyone behind any desk will be receptive to a variety of requests.

On the one hand, it makes sense that more students learn that there are different kinds of service available to them and make thoughtful and full use of those services. On the other hand, librarians may learn from students that some of the service divisions are simply unexamined holdovers from past times when they made sense. Now that a reference librarian needs little more than a networked computer with a screen that can swivel, and students are free to do research almost anywhere with a laptop and wireless access, why not position librarians where the patrons are? This might even include dorms.

Further, to make more of limited resources, librarians may want to explore opportunities to join forces with others in the university, such as IT or learning services staff, or even circulation staff or student workers. This is not to suggest that a student can provide the same level of service as a reference librarian. But perhaps it would help to have multiple staff at the same desk who then refer students to each other, as appropriate. Student workers can solve technology problems, provide directions, and answer straightforward reference questions, leaving librarians free to address the more complex or difficult questions or give their time to those students whose projects or interest levels merit it.

This is not to say that librarians should bend to every undergraduate whim and misperception. Sometimes understanding students leads to better ways to enlighten them and help them build skill and knowledge. For example, we have learned in our research that students look to their professors as the preeminent authorities on research paper resources (see Chapter 2). But we also know that faculty members are often poor users of such finding aids as online library catalogs and databases (Barry 1997; see Chapter 1). This suggests the value to librarians of pursuing better partnerships with teaching faculty, so that professors invite librarians into

their departments and classrooms and explicitly direct their students to approach librarians for bibliographic support.

Students tend to be overly confident of their self-service skills in the library arena (see Chapter 2). A student who cannot find resources for her/his paper assumes that the library simply does not have the resources. The student may resolve this problem by consulting Wikipedia or an unwarranted website; as long as their references are acceptable to their instructors, we can expect this practice to continue. Google does not, however, always lead students to the wealth of warranted information licensed by their institutions or in their own collections, and Wikipedia is not considered a reliable source by scholars (Read 2006a, b, c; Schiff 2006). If they make heavy use of Google and Wikipedia, social science and humanities students with serious academic interests may fail to develop the habits of mind, the skills, and the attitudes they will need to succeed in the academy (see Abbott 2006). Now as in the past, librarians have special expertise in finding resources; what has changed is that indexes are now online (Bell 2006). If more faculty members understood the changing nature of librarian expertise, they could help their students get better help.

Students may want Mommy, but that does not mean that the library should mother its students. There are students who will never do more than the minimum, and nothing will benefit them quite so much as simple searches that really work. And there is much to learn from student behavior and expectations about those aspects of libraries and their technologies that are simply outmoded. We might not want our students to use Google all the time, but giving them Google-like simplicity in the library interface—on top of functionality that supports precision searching and advanced forms of browsing—would certainly be desirable.

We are all the Millennial Generation now. The difference between today's college students and today's librarians is not the technology we use or the way we schedule our days. The difference is that a 50-year-old librarian has lived through several "generations," experienced different ways of doing things, and ended up older and wiser in this world, in this year, to deal with the same reality that confronts our youth. The 18- or 20-year-old student has less experience of generational change and depends on past generations to understand the past that created this world and this age. It is exactly the information of past generations that the library provides, often in writing, sometimes onscreen, and even in person.

Librarians can play a significant role in challenging students to develop their information-seeking skills and their judgment. This will help students become better citizens even if they have no intention of becoming researchers or academics. Librarians can share their insights about students with instructors, supporting faculty efforts to coordinate what happens in the library with what happens in the classroom; librarians can also contribute to a broader, ongoing consideration of the curriculum. It is the educational mission of the university and society's higher purposes that shape the role of the library and the work of librarians. Those who articulate that mission can learn from librarians about the real lives, the perspectives, and the potential of the students whom librarians know so well.

eleven. Conclusion: Creating Student-Centered Academic Libraries

Susan Gibbons and Nancy Fried Foster

The Undergraduate Research Project produced hundreds of pages of transcripts, dozens of photos, stacks of maps and drawings, and other artifacts that we can mine again and again for insights into the academic practices of our students. Staff from different parts of the University of Rochester River Campus Libraries joined together to engage in project activities, forming new bonds through a shared experience. The project has been an enormous success and we have already begun to use our insights to implement improvements in our libraries' services, facilities, and Web presence.

In our book, we have presented some of the more useful methods that produced this success and some of our most interesting data and interpretations. In conclusion, this final chapter provides an answer to our research question, discusses the meaning of our user-centered approach to design, and reflects on how the project affected the library as an organization.

How Students *Really* Write Their Papers

With regard to our central question—What do students *really* do when they write research papers?—we found a range of approaches and strategies, which we characterize with reference to a few real students. We prefer not to give a composite or average, since there is no composite or average student; there are only real students with quirky, evolving work practices. The following students—whose descriptions are slightly anonymized and whose identities are protected by the use of pseudonyms—provide four representative approaches to the writing of the research paper.

Abbie is an outstanding student with a history of school success. As a high school student, she became comfortable asking librarians for personal assistance and attention, a habit she brought with her to college. Abbie has maintained a weekly appointment with a tutor at the writing center despite her excellent organizational and writing skills, just to get that extra bit of help. She describes herself as an excellent student and says she works hard on her papers—and the rest of her academic work—because she is good at it. She has many genuine intellectual interests, including her major, which is preparing her to work in a field she finds worthwhile and personally satisfying. Abbie approaches her assignments by scheduling her research and writing activities, sometimes using a course syllabus and other times creating her own timeline. She is oriented to achievement and works hard to meet deadlines while driving herself to gather and digest extensive resources. She has learned to find published resources, whether print or electronic. She also makes use of a large personal network, developed through internships and travel, that includes students from around the world. She readily consults these overseas students for lo-

Susan Gibbons is Associate Dean, Public Services and Collection Development at the River Campus Libraries, University of Rochester; e-mail: sgibbons@library.rochester.edu. Nancy Fried Foster is Lead Anthropologist at the River Campus Libraries, University of Rochester; e-mail: nfoster@library.rochester.edu

cal, up-to-date information on her topics. Abbie is a hardworking student who says that she feels internally motivated to learn and externally motivated to gain further educational and travel opportunities. She is a passionate learner.

Danielle is a diligent student who extends her generally cheerful attitude to her courses and instructors. She enjoys many of the habits of the idler, such as television viewing and shopping. Her academic habits are not altogether different. She takes pleasure in browsing the library bookshelves, almost like a flâneur in the stacks. She also enjoys selecting and using paper, pens, and notebooks—that is, she appreciates the materiality of her academic work. Danielle participates wholeheartedly in college, and for her it is a life—a full, rounded, integrated experience. She approaches her papers as one might the preparation of a meal: reviewing the recipe, gathering the ingredients—enjoying the aroma, color, texture, and taste of each—and then combining them into an artfully arranged dish. She is a gourmet.

Brandon is a pretty good student who has never liked the library. He has strong interests outside of his academics and a set of friends who share those interests. Indeed, he finds himself torn between his academics and other pastimes, including a variety of sports and games. Brandon good-naturedly attends classes and finds resources to complete assignments, although he would probably do something else if an assignment were not due. Despite this somewhat lackadaisical attitude, Brandon is genuinely interested in many of his classes, enjoys much of his reading, and loves the variety of disciplines and areas of study that college opens up to him. Brandon's approach to a paper is to go through the steps, asking peers—but never a librarian—for help when he needs it, and continuing to work until he is done. He is oriented to living life; his education, while enjoyable, is instrumental—a ticket to what comes next.

Tiffany finds it hard to maintain passing grades. She dislikes the library as a physical place and avoids the library website. She feels that she made a mistake coming to this college because it is so hard for her to succeed in her classes. Tiffany's nonacademic interests clearly outweigh her academic ones, and she shows little enthusiasm for her college courses and little interest in mastering course material or other intellectual work for any reason. She has no regular approach to writing papers and little inclination to stake out a position and argue it consistently. Tiffany seems like a bystander to her own education.

These are only four students, and they are not archetypes or averages; they are real individuals. They do not sum up or typify all students, but they give us some insight on representative characteristics and gross differences among our students. These and many other students engage, with more or less success, in a range of paper-writing activities, which may include these:

- Reviewing the requirements
- Consulting with the professor or instructor about the requirements, the topic, or resources
- Consulting with others about the topic and resources (this may include librarians, friends, family members, or student workers in the library)
- Creating a timeline or adding the assigned timeline to a planner
- Choosing a topic and consulting preliminary resources to do so
- Gathering resources through the library, Google, the professor or instructor, friends and family, and other sources
- Making notes
- Creating a bibliography or an annotated bibliography
- Creating an outline
- Completing and submitting research-relat-

ed class assignments, as required (e.g., topic statements, bibliographies, early drafts)

- Meeting with the professor or instructor, a writing tutor, a librarian, or another expert, as needed
- Composing the paper in sections, or free form, or following a strict outline, or writing it all in one extended work session, as one's particular practices and preferences dictate
- Asking others to read and comment on the paper, or proofread the paper; this may include peers, a writing tutor, or parents
- Revising the paper, seeking additional resources, and checking details as required
- Completing the bibliography; this may entail the use of RefWorks, EndNote, or another digital bibliographic tool
- Submitting the final version either on paper or electronically

Although this series of steps seems obvious, some of the details surprised us. For example, we were all surprised at the extent to which students consult their parents and other family members about their academic work. We were also surprised that students have such a narrow view of what librarians can do for them (find books on shelves, locate items they already know about) and such strong feelings that faculty members, and faculty members only, are experts at finding good scholarly resources. We were also surprised to find that students are on average no more proficient with computer technology than librarians or faculty members. Some students demonstrated broad knowledge of computers and facility in using them, but others were awkward and clumsy. And one of the biggest surprises was that many students feel enchained by that technology and struggle to break free, especially of instant messaging and similar distractions.

Every student has a unique approach to writing papers. Our research has allowed us to understand the work habits of some representative students and to get a sense of the broad variation across the large group of research participants. Our research has also allowed us to recalibrate our sense of our students and how their experiences relate to our own. Although many aspects of the college experience have changed and are unlike the experiences librarians remember from their own college days, there is still much in common between student and librarian lives. We all use the latest technologies, although students tend to use them more. We all want to meet our own information needs, although students are more confident—sometimes overconfident—of their abilities and less comfortable seeking certain kinds of expert advice. We are all busy, although they are more likely to push their academic work into the nighttime hours when they are alone with a network connection to a database. We are all keeping our options open, although students do not really know what their options are, or which options might be best, or how to organize themselves to do what they want now and get where they want to go in the future. We would do better to understand our students' lives not in terms of our own college experiences but in terms of our own current lives. They are not really so different from us except that they are kids, newly set loose on the world.

User-Centered Design

User-centered design means designing things—technology, spaces, services—to meet the needs of the people who will use them and to perform well in real-life situations. In a university, user-centered design is not entirely straightforward. When we design for students, we design for people whose practices and preferences may be at odds with the university's educational mission or their instructors' demands. So user-centered design in higher education must take a broad view of the "user" and pay attention to a wide range of needs, preferences, and constraints on the part of numerous people who are served by the technology, spaces, and services the library provides.

Throughout our project, we collected information about student work practices without evaluating those practices. This is part of the method: to observe everything, take it all in, and understand it without rushing into judgment or problem solving. However, once we have made extensive observations and amassed a large set of data, we must interpret it in the relevant context. We are designing technology, spaces, and services for an academic library, not a summer camp, a fitness center, or an airport. Students may want to eat in the library, socialize in the library, and sleep in the library, and we may want to make that possible. But they can do those things elsewhere. There are some things they can *only* do in the library; those things must have priority.

When students draw an ideal library space and the drawing includes a massage room, our response is not to run out and buy almond oil. We understand the massage room to represent the student's need to feel comfortable or to feel that s/he belongs in the space. We might meet that need by providing comfortable chairs or by making sure that students can easily understand signs and directions, so that they know they are where they should be. And so on.

Our aim is to understand how students work and how they might work better so that they can reach the standards set by the faculty and so that the university can work toward its mission. Once we understand this, we set about to support the work practices that will help our students, and the library and the university, succeed. This, for us, is user-centered design.

Organizational Change

Some people use the long and glorious history of academic libraries as proof that academic libraries will have an equally long and glorious future.

This supports the view that libraries should keep services, collections, and facilities much as they are. It often requires a significant event to change the culture of an organization and disrupt the status quo; the Undergraduate Research Project appears to be such an event for the River Campus Libraries.

The project was a wake-up call. We saw over and over again how much we did not know about our students and their academic endeavors. But, perhaps more important, we saw how often our personal assumptions about the students, which have guided years of decisions, were incorrect. We tend to assume that our own student experiences are largely similar to those of our students, but as Chapters 9 and 10 illustrate, this is not the case. As an organization, we must be suspicious of any declaration that begins, "When I was in college…"

Engaging in an extended research project has fostered an experimental spirit among the staff. New, creative ideas are emerging all across the organization, at all levels. Although ours has always been a creative staff, what seems different is that the ideas are being tried and explored, largely without the need to form committees and seek approval from all levels of the organizational hierarchy. Instead, the more bureaucratic necessities enter in only after a mini-experiment proves promising. In addition, members of our library staff have become more tolerant of the risks associated with an experiment. Not every experiment will be a success, but from each there is information to be learned.

Having an anthropologist on staff has made it possible for library staff to learn many different techniques borrowed or adapted from a wide range of anthropological and ethnographic studies. It has also helped us develop a toolkit to use whenever we find ourselves with a question that we could answer if only we knew more about our students, our faculty members, or our own staff. After a learning period, more and more members of the library staff are gaining experience and competence in a range of research methods. Many of them now feel comfortable conducting some research activities on their own, without the presence or direct support of the anthropologist. We have come to understand and appreciate how easy it can sometimes be to talk to students and get information from them. The design workshops described in Chapters 4 and 5 are good examples of this. Organizationally, we are moving toward a shared mindset that, when it comes to what our students need and want from the libraries, "Don't guess, just ask."

Student-Centered Libraries

In recent years, a new phrase has entered the vocabulary of higher education administrators and their funding bodies: "student-centered." This new emphasis on students began in the classroom, with student-centered pedagogy and student-centered learning, but it has now spread across campus, so that today Google lists more than 13,000 results for "student-centered university." Consequently, it should come as no surprise that the concept of "student-centered libraries" has emerged.

To be truly student-centered requires a rather deep knowledge and understanding of today's undergraduate students. Fortunately, we have organizations such as EDUCAUSE, Pew Internet and American Life Project, and OCLC, which are conducting studies, surveys, and environmental scans of college students, such as the recent ECAR *Study of Undergraduate Students and Information Technology* (Salaway et al. 2006). It is from sources like this that we can start to see some high-level trends, including the importance of social networking sites (Lenhart and Madden 2007), the continued predominance of the association of the physical book with libraries (OCLC 2005), and the relegation of e-mail to communication with "old people" (Lenhart et al. 2005).

All the same, as useful as this information is, we must remember that these represent high-level trends and the aggregation of data from many higher education institutions. The reality is that the student body of each higher education institution is unique, for it is a reflection of a variety of factors including socioeconomic conditions, the ratio of residential to commuter students, local climate, and the robustness of the campus IT infrastructure, just to name a few. Consequently, to be truly student-centered we must be cognizant of the high-level student trends but truly fluent in the local campus situation.

The Undergraduate Research Project was our way of tapping into our local student environment and collecting data upon which to base our student-centered organization. Since the start of the project, we have made changes in reference services (Chapter 3), enlarged our partnership with the college writing center (Chapter 1), and altered library instruction. Support for all of these changes can be found in the student data we collected. The same can be said for the forthcoming changes to our library facilities (Chapter 4) and website (Chapter 5). As an organization, we can collectively turn to our data about students to inform decisions about services, resources, facilities, and our Web presence. When we find that the data are lacking, we can tap our toolkit of user research methodologies to find a way to gather the data we lack.

The River Campus Libraries' intent to be student-centered is decades old but was never fully realizable until we began to collect fine-grained ethnographic information about our students. The project has given us the tools and information to convert our intent into a reality, and to do so with confidence. The Undergraduate Research Project has helped us shape our organization into a truly student-centered library.

References

Abbott, Andrew. 2006. *The University library: Report of the task force on the university library*. http://www.lib.uchicago.edu/staff-web/groups/space/abbott-report.html.

Albanese, Andrew Richard. 2005. The best thing a library can be is open. *Library Journal* 130 (15): 42–44.

Alch, Mark L. 2000. The echo-boom generation: A growing force in American society. *Futurist* 34 (5): 42.

Alvarez, Barbara. 2007. *A new perspective on reference: Crossing the line between research and writing*. Paper presented at the 5th "Reference in the 21st-Century" Symposium at Columbia University. https://www1.columbia.edu/sec/cu/libraries/bts/img/assets/9337/Columbia%20paper.pdf.

Barnes & Noble Booksellers. n.d. *Barnes & Noble history*. http://www.barnesandnobleinc.com/our_company/history/bn_history.html.

Barry, Christine A. 1997. Information skills for an electronic world: Training doctoral research students. *Journal of Information Science* 23(3): 225–38.

Becker, Howard Saul, Blanche Geer, and Everett C. Hughes. 1968. *Making the grade: The academic side of college life*. New York: John Wiley and Sons.

Bell, Suzanne S. 2006. *Librarian's guide to online searching*. Westport, CT: Libraries Unlimited.

Beloit College. 2006. Mindset Lists. http://www.beloit.edu/~pubaff/mindset/.

Borders Group. n.d. *Our history*. http://www.bordersgroupinc.com/about/history.htm.

Briden, Judi, Vicki Burns, and Ann Marshall. 2007. Knowing our students: Undergraduates in context. In *Proceedings of the 2007 ACRL National Conference*, Baltimore, MD. http://docushare.lib.rochester.edu/docushare/dsweb/Get/Document-25072/Knowing_our_students_URochester.pdf.

Brun-Cottan, Francoise, and Patricia Wall. 1995. Using video to re-present the user. *Communications of the ACM* (Association for Computing Machinery) 38 (5): 61–72.

Carlson, Jake. 2006. An examination of undergraduate student citation behavior. *Journal of Academic Librarianship* 32 (1): 14–22.

Carlson, Scott. 2005. Net generation goes to college. *Chronicle of Higher Education* 52 (7): A34.

Davis, Philip M. 2003. Effect of the Web on undergraduate citation behavior: Guiding student scholarship in a networked age. *Portal: Libraries and the Academy* 3 (1): 41–51.

DeRosa, Cathy. 2006. *College students' perceptions of libraries and information resources.* Dublin, OH: OCLC Online Computer Library Center, http://www.oclc.org/reports/perceptionscollege.htm.

Foley, James A., and Robert K. Foley. 1969. *The college scene: Students tell it like it is.* New York: Cowles Book Company.

Foster, Nancy Fried, and Susan Gibbons. 2005. Understanding faculty to improve content recruitment for institutional repositories, *D-Lib Magazine* 11 (1). http://www.dlib.org/dlib/january05/foster/01foster.html. See also Grey Literature/DSpace Project: Shared Results http://tinyurl.com/jufm2.

Gardner, Ralph Jr. 2006. In college, you can go home again and again. *New York Times,* December 14, G9.

Gaver, Bill, Tony Dunne, and Elena Pacenti. 1999. Design: Cultural probes. *Interactions* 6 (1): 21–29.

Gee, James Paul. 2003. *What video games have to teach us about learning and literacy.* New York: Palgrave Macmillan.

Greenfield, Mark A. 2006. *Born to be wired: Technology, communication, and the millennial generation.* Paper presented to the Laboratory for Laser Energetics, University of Rochester. http://wings.buffalo.edu/provost/webserveces/presentations/highedwebdev2005/highedweb2006public.ppt.

Gross, Daniel R. 1984. Time allocation: A tool for the study of cultural behavior. *Annual Review of Anthropology* 13:519–58.

Harper, Douglas. 1984. Meaning and work: A study in photo elicitation. *International Journal of Visual Sociology* 2 (1): 20–43.

———. 2001. *Changing works: Visions of a lost agriculture.* Chicago: University of Chicago Press.

———. 2006. *Good company: A tramp life.* Boulder: Paradigm Publishers.

Howe, Neil, and William Strauss. 2003. *Millennials go to college: Strategies for a new generation on campus: Recruiting and admissions, campus life, and the classroom.* Washington, DC: American Association of College Registrars and Admissions.

Kaplan, Isabel. 2006. *Mapping diaries and design workshops.* Paper presented at Internet Librarian 2006, Monterey, CA.

Kvavik, Robert B. 2005. Convenience, communications, and control: How students use technology. In *Educating the net generation,* ed. Diana G. Oblinger and James L. Oblinger. Boulder, CO: EDUCAUSE. http://www.educause.edu/ir/library/pdf/PUB7101G.pdf.

Lenhart, Amanda, and Mary Madden. 2007. *Social networking websites and teens: An overview.* Washington, DC: Pew Internet and American Life Project. http://www.pewinternet.org/pdfs/PIP_SNS_Data_Memo_Jan_2007.pdf.

Lenhart, Amanda, Mary Madden, and Paul Hitlin. 2005. *Teens and technology: Youth are leading the transition to a fully wired and mobile nation.* Washington, DC: Pew Internet and American Life Project. http://www.pewinternet.org/pdfs/PIP_Teens_Tech_July2005web.pdf.

Lomas, Cyprien, and Diane G. Oblinger. 2006. Student practices and their impact on learning spaces. In *Learning Spaces*, ed. Diane G. Oblinger. Boulder, CO: EDUCAUSE. http://www.educause.edu/ir/library/pdf/PUB7102e.pdf.

Marshall, Ann. 2006. *Lining up research paper support: The roles of librarians and writing tutors*. Paper presented at the Conference on College Composition and Communication, Chicago, March 22–25.

McGlynn, Angela Provitera. 2005. Teaching millennials, our newest cultural cohort. *Education Digest* 71 (4): 12–16.

McMillan, Sally J., and Margaret Morrison. 2006. Coming of age with the Internet: A qualitative exploration of how the Internet has become an integral part of young people's lives. *New Media and Society* 8 (1): 73–95.

Mitchell, Susan. 2000. *American generations: Who they are. How they live. What they think.* 3d ed. Ithaca, NY: New Strategist Publications.

Moffatt, Michael. 1989. *Coming of age in New Jersey: College and American culture.* New Brunswick: Rutgers University Press.

———. 1991. College life: Undergraduate culture and higher education. *Journal of Higher Education* 62 (1): 44–61.

Nathan, Rebekah. 2005. My freshman year: What a professor learned by becoming a student. Ithaca, NY: Cornell University Press.

Oblinger, Diane G. 2003. Boomers, Gen-Xers, Millennials: Understanding the new students. *EDUCAUSE Review* 38 (4): 37–45.

Oblinger, Diana, and James Oblinger. 2005. Is it age or IT: First steps towards understanding the Net Generation. In *Educating the Net Generation,* ed. Diana G. Oblinger and James Oblinger. Boulder, CO: EDUCAUSE. http://www.educause.edu/ir/library/pdf/pub7101b.pdf.

Prensky, Marc. 2001. Digital natives, digital immigrants. *On the Horizon* 9 (5): 1–6.

Rainie, L. 2006. *Life online: Teens and technology and the world to come.* Speech ed. http://www.pewinternet.org/ppt/Teens%20and%20technology.pdf.

Read, Brock. 2004. Have you "Facebooked" him? *Chronicle of Higher Education* 50 (38): A29.

———. 2006a. Can Wikipedia ever make the grade? *Chronicle of Higher Education* 53 (10): A31.

———. 2006b. Students flock to an easy-to-use reference, but professors warn that it's no sure thing. *Chronicle of Higher Education* 53(10): A36.

———. 2006c. Middlebury College history department limits students' use of Wikipedia. *Chronicle of Higher Education* 53 (24): A39.

Reference and Users Service Association. 2007. *Guidelines for behavioral performance of reference and information service providers.* http://www.ala.org/ala/rusa/rusaprotools/referenceguide/guidelinesbehavioral.htm.

Ricker, Shirley, and Isabel Kaplan. 2006. *Are we crossing the line? A survey of library and writing program collaboration.* Paper presented at the Conference on College Composition and Communication, Chicago, March 22–25. http://docushare.lib.rochester.edu/docushare/dsweb/Get/Document-22020/Library_Writing_Collaboration.pdf.

Roper, Shannon L., and Jeannette Kindred. 2005. IM here: Reflections on virtual office hours. *First Monday* 10 (11). http://www.firstmonday.org/issues/issue10_11/roper/index.html.

Sabar, Ariel. 2006. Backstory: Look, Mom, it's me. I'm OK! *Christian Science Monitor*, December 4. http://www.csmonitor.com/2006/1204/p20s01-legn.html.

Sanford, Nevitt. (ed.). 1962. *The American college: A psychological and social interpretation of the higher learning.* New York: John Wiley & Sons.

Schiff, Stacy. 2006. Know it all. *New Yorker,* July 31, 36.

Singh, Annmarie B. 2005. A report on faculty perceptions of students' information literacy competencies in journalism and mass communication programs: The ACEJMC survey. *College and Research Libraries* 66 (4): 294–310.

Suchman, Lucy A., and Randall H. Trigg. 1991. Understanding practice: Video as a medium for reflection and design. In *Design at work: Cooperative design of computer systems,* ed. Joan Greenbaum and Morten Kyng, 65–89. Hillsdale, NJ: Lawrence Erlbaum Associates.

Taubenek, Anne. 2006. The Millennials: Always on. *Northwestern Magazine.* http://www.northwestern.edu/magazine/summer2006/cover/millenials.html

Thomas, Chuck, and Robert H. McDonald. 2005. *Millennial net value(s): Disconnects between libraries and the information age mindset.* Tallahassee: Florida State University Libraries. http://dscholarship.lib.fsu.edu/general/4.

Toffler, Alvin. 1970. Future shock. New York: Random House.

Twenge, Jean M. 2006. Generation me: Why today's young Americans are more confident, assertive, entitled—and more miserable than ever before. New York: Free Press.

Valentine, Barbara. 2001. The legitimate effort in research papers: Student commitment versus faculty expectations. *Journal of Academic Librarianship* 27 (2): 107–15.

Wagner, Cynthia G. 2006. Blabbing on your blog. *Futurist* 40 (4): 7

Washington-Hoagland, Carlette, and Leo Clougherty. 2002. Identifying the resource and service needs of graduate and professional students: The University of Iowa user needs of graduate professional series. *Portal: Libraries and the Academy* 2 (1): 125–43.

Wilder, Stanley J. 2003. *Demographic change in academic librarianship.* Washington, DC: Association of Research Libraries.

———. 2005. Unpublished data. Association of Research Libraries. Washington, DC.

Young, Jeffrey R. 2006. The fight for classroom attention: Professor vs. laptop. *Chronicle of Higher Education* 52 (39): A27.

Authors

Barbara Alvarez is a reference librarian and subject librarian for Modern Languages and Cultures in Rush Rhees Library, University of Rochester. Besides working at the reference desk, she provides bibliographic instruction, manages foreign language and literature collections, participates in several digital initiatives, and forms part of the River Campus Libraries' usability team. Barbara holds an MA in Hispanic literatures and an MLIS, both earned at the University of Alberta, Canada. Before joining the Reference Department at Rochester in 2001, she worked as a reference librarian and Spanish language instructor at the University of Alberta.

Helen Anderson is Head, Collection Development, and subject librarian for Russian Studies at the River Campus Libraries. Prior to joining the University of Rochester she was Slavic and East European Studies librarian, then Head of the Humanities and Social Sciences Collections Department at McGill University Libraries. Helen provides leadership for River Campus Libraries' subject librarians program. She presented a talk titled "Subject Librarians, Collection Development and the Culture of Assessment" at ARL's Library Assessment Conference in September 2006.

Suzanne Bell has been a librarian and educator for many years, holding a variety of subject librarian and instruction positions at several institutions. She is currently the librarian for economics and data in the Reference Department of the Rush Rhees Library at the University of Rochester. She has been an adjunct instructor for the University of Buffalo Library School and is the author of *The Librarian's Guide to Online Searching*, published in 2006.

Judi Briden is Digital Librarian for Public Services at the University of Rochester, River Campus Libraries. She leads the libraries' metasearch group, advises on content and design for the libraries' Web redesign project, and serves on the Mellon-funded eXtensible Catalog project team. She is the subject librarian for Brain and Cognitive Sciences and the American Sign Language Program. She earned an MLIS from the University of Texas at Austin.

Vicki Burns is Head, Rush Rhees Reference Department, and the subject librarian for Anthropology and Sociology at the University of Rochester, River Campus Libraries. Currently she is leading the libraries' Web redesign project team. Prior to her current position she was head of the Management Library. Before joining the University of Rochester Libraries, Ms. Burns managed a technical library for Mobil Chemical in Macedon, New York.

Katie Clark is the Somerville Director of the Science and Engineering Libraries at the University of Rochester. In addition to working at the University of Rochester, she has held positions at the University of Houston, Pennsylvania State University, and Texas A&M University libraries. She has an MLS and MS from the University of Hawaii and an AB from Mount Holyoke College. Katie has been an active member of the ACRL Science and Technology Section of ALA for almost two decades.

Nora Dimmock is head of the Multimedia Center and subject librarian for Film and Media Studies for the University of Rochester, River Campus Libraries. She is an active member of the libraries' usability team and the College Diversity Roundtable. Her research interests include usability, digital copyright issues, and popular culture collections in academic libraries.

Nancy Fried Foster is Lead Anthropologist for the River Campus Libraries and manager of the digital initiatives unit. She is a principal investigator on both an IMLS-funded study of next-generation repository users and the eXtensible Catalog project, which is funded by the Mellon Foundation. She has conducted studies on research and library practices of faculty and students as well as several small studies of librarian work practices. With a PhD in applied anthropology, Dr. Foster has extensive research experience in the Amazon and Papua New Guinea as well as in educational and other institutions in the United States and United Kingdom. She has received Fulbright, Woodrow Wilson, and Spencer Foundation grants for her anthropological research projects.

Sarada W. George is a library assistant at Carlson Science and Engineering Library at the University of Rochester. She has a BA from Brandeis University and an MA from the University of Rochester. She has previously taught psychology at Nazareth College of Rochester and served as volunteer librarian at the Montessori School of Rochester.

Susan Gibbons is Associate Dean for Public Services and Collection Development for the River Campus Libraries, University of Rochester. She earned an MLS and MA in history from Indiana University, a professional MBA from the University of Massachusetts, and is currently working on her doctorate in higher education administration.

She held library positions at Indiana University and University of Massachusetts, Amherst, before moving to the University of Rochester, where she worked as the director of digital library initiatives prior to joining the River Campus Libraries' administration. She was named one of *Library Journal*'s 2005 "Movers & Shakers" and was a 2006 Visiting Program Officer for the Association for Research Libraries.

Kenn Harper is a reference librarian for the Carlson Science and Engineering Library and the Laser Lab Library at the University of Rochester. He is also currently subject librarian for biology, laser fusion, and mechanical engineering and served as the Physics/Optics/Astronomy librarian at the University of Rochester. Before coming to Rochester in 1990 he worked in public services at the University of Michigan and the Oregon Health and Science University. Kenn has a BS in biology from Ohio State University as well as an MS in zoology and an MLIS from the University of Michigan.

Ann Marshall is a reference librarian and the Political Science subject librarian at Rush Rhees Library, University of Rochester. She received her MLS from Syracuse University's School of Information Studies and an MA in political science and PhD in the social science program, both from Syracuse University's Maxwell School of Citizenship and Public Affairs. She is an active member of the Law and Political Science Section of the ACRL.

Jane McCleneghan Smith is a 30-year member of the Acquisitions Department, Rush Rhees Library, where she is responsible for ordering materials in all formats from publishers and vendors worldwide. She has served on and chaired library committees and presented papers at local and state library conferences. In her academic life, Mrs. Smith has a Master's degree in German from Northwestern University and has taught courses at the University of Rochester and the Rochester Institute of Technology. She has published translations of essays by Agnes Heller and Ludwig von Mises. In addition to German, Mrs. Smith's knowledge of Spanish, French, and Italian support her work in the Acquisitions Department.

Alan Unsworth grew up in Ithaca, New York, and attended colleges in three different states. His favorite was the University of Washington, Seattle, where he earned degrees in ancient and medieval history and library science. He is the History subject librarian at Rush Rhees Library, University of Rochester.

Printed in the United States
95204LV00004B/1-300/A

6932